UNDERHANDED
BACKGAMMON

UNDERHANDED BACKGAMMON

A Devious Guide to the Art
of Backhanded Backgammon

ARTHUR PRAGER

Illustrated by Roy Schlemme

HAWTHORN BOOKS, INC.
PUBLISHERS/*New York*

UNDERHANDED BACKGAMMON

Library of Congress Catalog Card Number: 76-15764

ISBN: 0-8015-8125-7

1 2 3 4 5 6 7 8 9 10

Contents

UNDERHANDED BACKGAMMON

1
Introduction: Between the Lines

Backgammon, as James Houghfflin pointed out in his *Treatise on the Strategies of Backgammon and Other War Games*, was originally designed to train young soldiers in the art of combat. Throughout its five-thousand-year history, the game has equipped both tyrants and benevolent rulers alike with the required know-how for wiping out whole civilizations. Someday, perhaps, a history will be written of the untold millions of men, women, and children annihilated and the cultures curtailed by what was merely an off-the-board "lover's leap" or by some skillful general fatefully ordering his troops to "send them to the bar!"

It seems ironic that a game designed for predators should emerge in the 1970's as a popular and friendly pastime, a peaceful and pleasurable activity for occupying cozy evenings before the fire or romantic afternoons on idyllic summer beaches. But is the game as peaceful as it looks, or does it retain a few traces of its bloodthirsty history? It is to answer that question that this book has been written.

Research into the history of the game reveals that the Romans adored backgammon, calling it *ludus duodecim scriptorum,* or the "twelve line game." Plato mentions it in the tenth book of *The Republic,* in which he refers to a game in which men were moved according to the casting of dice. Chaucer mentions a *ludus Anglicorum* in the Harleian MSS of 1527, in which he described "tables" on which men were moved back and forth according to the roll of three dice, one of which was imaginary and was always assumed to have rolled a six. And, of course, what we call Russian backgammon was a favorite of French kings under its nickname of *tric-trac.*

The pseudonymous Edwardian writer Berkeley remarked in his treatise on the game, "Backgammon has always been considered a particularly respectable kind of amusement, quite fitting for country rectors, and not derogatory to the dignity of even higher functionaries of the Church."* To that sentiment he added, "It is only persons of consequence who play at Backgammon, and those only who are the most quick-witted, ready, and watchful can ever thoroughly master it."

Berkeley was quite right about the need for quick wits and vigilance, although there may be some debate about his applying the adjective "respectable" to the game. Furthermore, he was not quite accurate in his assessment of backgammon as being played only by "persons of consequence." Over the years the game ceased to be a pastime for the upper classes and filtered down the social scale until by the 1920's almost every household in the civilized world had a backgammon board. Of course, most people didn't know they had one, for in those days it was customary to print backgammon points, or *fléches,* on the backs of checkerboards.

---

*Berkeley, *Draughts and Backgammon* (New York: G. Bell & Sons, 1911), p. 80.

I must confess that I, a passionate checker player at the age of six, wondered what could possibly be the purpose of those two-dozen, long, thin triangles on the back of my cardboard board. With a boy's simple logic I assumed that they were for coloring and utilized them accordingly.

Whatever the origins of the game and the implications of its evolving history, it is hard to play backgammon merely for fun. The game is designed for gambling, whether for high stakes or low, and any game in which one player can remove property from another by a combination of strategy and luck can be deadly. In other words, remember Berkeley's caution to be ready and watchful, or you might tumble into some of the pitfalls I have described in this volume, as did the unfortunates about whom you will read in the ensuing chapters.

Remember that in all combative pastimes (backgammon included), strategy depends heavily on full knowledge of the psychology of one's opponent.

Remember, too, Troy's passion for homemade wooden horses.

But more about that in a moment.

2
Know Your Rabbit

I learned a valuable lesson one muggy summer day in New York's Greenwich Village, home of intellectuals, poets, and eccentrics of all sorts. It was a lesson that I have been able to apply to sessions of backgammon, and I have never forgotten it. Moreover, since instruction is the purpose of this book, I have no objection whatsoever to sharing it with you.

Lessons of the Silver Screen

It began when I met Sasha Schreiber.

I first saw him at a backgammon seminar held at the New School for Social Research on Eleventh Street. He sat ramrod straight, paying fierce attention to everything that was said. When he agreed with a point of information, he nodded rapidly so that his wiry, shoulder-length ponytail bobbed up and down. Sunlight beaming through the window flashed on his circular steel-rimmed glasses. Occasionally, he muttered something unintelligible under his breath. I could not tell whether it was in approval or disagreement with the speaker's thesis. Nevertheless, I was fascinated by his long, thin nose, the skin of which stretched tightly over the bone, leaving a small white circle at the tip. At this first meeting he appeared to be deeply absorbed in the discussion. At one point, I saw his body stiffen when the speaker, a fussy and opinionated young woman in an orange dashiki, said in no uncertain terms that the word *backgammon* was derived from the Saxon *bacc* for "back" and *gamen* for "game." A game in which the pieces are "sent back."

Shaking his head in lofty disapproval, Sasha muttered, *"back cammaun,"* loudly enough for me to hear, indicating that he favored the early Welsh literal translation, "little battle."

"Bakke gammen," I whispered in the direction of his large pointed ear, revealing myself as a proponent of the ancient Danish hypothesis, the words derived from the Scandinavian and meaning "tray game."

He turned and gave me a look of shrewd appraisal.

After the class was over and the other students had drifted away, I suggested that we share coffee at a nearby establishment. He accepted, and in due course we became friends, meeting periodically to discuss our favorite subject. Finally, after some coyness on both sides, one of us (I don't remember which) suggested a game. We have been playing backgammon regularly ever since.

Sasha was a fanatic. He played brilliantly, contemptuously, with little or no patience for fools. If I made a move he disapproved of or which, to his way of thinking, was inferior to another available move, he would emit a little compressed-air sound from between his narrowed lips. A kind of "ptooh," like a man expelling a watermelon seed, indicating that such a move was unthinkable.

As a rule I disagreed with him, but quite often he turned out to be right. He had the ability common to many expert chess players of foreseeing the next four or five moves that

7

would inevitably follow a given move, allowing for the possible variations of intelligence or luck. Of course, even the most skillful backgammon player can be unhorsed by an unfortunate roll of the dice, but in the long run, the more experienced, better-trained strategist will win. Combine those qualities with native brilliance and a certain dashing willingness to take risks, and, well—Sasha marched over me again and again like the proverbial army with banners.

Sasha is your die-hard, never-give-an-inch type. He has the uncanny knack of saying very little while letting the whole world know that only through socialism will true salvation come. His conversation bristles with references to Kierkegaard and Max Brod. I once overheard a little dialogue he was having with a wide-eyed young girl in which he referred to Franz Kafka and Rainer Maria Rilke as Frank and Ray. She was terribly impressed.

One evening, as a change and to whet our appetites for our more-or-less friendly game, Sasha and I decided to go to a movie. We strolled down Sullivan Street toward Bleecker, he in his traditional-patterned ankle socks and Braun sandals, sporting a sweatshirt that warned all citizens to abjure the temptations of California grapes, and I in somewhat more conservative attire. The film was a Brian DePalma effort called *Get to Know Your Rabbit*.

It was a splendidly simple story about a tap-dancing magician who starts his theatrical career in the cocktail lounges and bowling alleys of the middle-American outback, all the while trying to improve his dexterity and luck. At one juncture in the action, the hero's mentor (an older and more successful illusionist) tells him that in order to perfect the art of sleight-of-hand or, in short, to pull a rabbit effectively out of a hat, one must first know one's rabbit. Absorbing the lesson, the young fellow moves on to stardom and comes away as the proud possessor of the knack, the rabbit, and, of course, the girl.

To me, sitting in the darkened theatre, it made a good deal of sense. By simple transposition I was able to apply the same lesson to backgammon. For example, when I played with Sasha, I always made a valiant effort to play *his* game—cold, audacious, brilliant. And I always lost. I was playing the part of his rabbit, waiting patiently in my tight, dark corner until he chose to seize me by the ears, pull me out, and make me perform.

But suppose I used his psychology and turned it against him—made him *my* rabbit, so to speak. Would that change matters? I knew I had as much experience and as much knowledge of the game as he did. Basically, I played as well as he did, but somehow when we bent over the board in his cluttered living room, he always won.

From now on things would be different.

Back in Sasha's flat after the movie, we laid out the board and positioned the men. A light rain pattered against the window panes, cooling the humid July air. A faint breeze ballooned his dusty curtains. Sasha surveyed the board grimly through narrowed lids. A king-size cigarette was clamped between his thin lips. Sasha's cigarettes always made me nervous. The ash would grow longer and longer, never dropping off on his chest until every ganglion in my body was screaming, "Fall! Fall!" At the last minute, he would calmly deposit the ash in an ashtray and light a new cigarette.

I was to learn on later acquaintance that before starting a game, Sasha always inserted an ordinary needle down the length of his cigarette. It creates a kind of armature to which the ash clings. If this is done, a cigarette ash will often reach a length of two inches or more before it falls, driving the smoker's companion out of his mind with anxiety and thus preventing him or her from devoting full attention to matters at hand. However, that is beside the point. This time, intent on trying my new strategy, I ignored the cigarette.

9

A cigarette ash will often reach a length of two inches or more before driving the smoker's companion crazy.

As the game progressed, I could see that my absolute calm was beginning to rattle Sasha. To his way of thinking, I was not taking the contest seriously enough. I even ventured a little secret smile from time to time. It froze him. Obviously I was up to something, but what? He watched me closely, assessing my play to see what my strategy might be.

At last we approached the end game of a match on which a moderate wager was riding and in which Sasha had confidently but with some surprise accepted a double. I could see he expected to win without too much trouble. I rolled the dice, and in their usual tricky manner, they presented me with a decision. I could make a standard move that would advance my game to a certain degree, thereby improving my chance of winning. Or I could make a stupid move, leaving two strategically-placed blots in danger of being sent to the bar, a serious setback. It was time for my rabbit.

I made the stupid move.

Sasha started back as though I had struck him. The ash from his cigarette dropped prematurely to the floor where the needle stuck, quivering.

"What do you think you're doing?" he demanded angrily.

"What do you mean what do I think I'm doing?"

"I mean if you want to play backgammon, play backgammon. If you don't want to play, we won't play."

"I want to play backgammon."

"Then what . . .?" He stopped suddenly and stared at the board. A small vein pulsed in his temple. His nose whitened with tension. I could see his reasoning process as clearly as if his head had been one of those educational toys labeled "The Human Brain at Work."

Since he himself was a consummate trickster and a keen, incisive strategist, he naturally assumed that his opponent was the same. Obviously, what I had done was some sort of trick. Shrewd as he was, he could not accept the possibility that before his very eyes, an opponent of his was capable of stupidity, and stupidity, moreover, garnished with a smile of undaunted confidence rather than a shamefaced apology.

If my move was a trick, it was obvious that I intended him to hit my two blots if possible. The odds certainly leaned in that direction. Therefore, I must have some master plan that could be unleashed if they were sent to the bar. Intelligent fellow that he was, he would show me that he wasn't to be taken in by anything so elementary.

In a lordly manner he rolled and although the dice permitted him to hit my blots almost at once, he made alternative moves. In a few minutes I had moved them off the board. A little later I won the game and pocketed the stakes.

I had made Sasha my rabbit. Using his own psychology, when the time was ripe, I pulled him out of a symbolic hat and made him perform according to my rules.

He couldn't believe it. He refused to accept the fact that he had fallen into an easy trap. After all, I had won the game. There *had* to be some master strategy in my last moves. From that game on, until he moved to a commune up near Stockbridge, Massachusetts, Sasha played like a madman in his games with me. He lost most of the time.

On several occasions at the New School, I saw him sitting alone, a traveling board open before him, with the men arranged as they had been during that fateful contest, working out the odds on possible permutations of the dice, like a man solving a difficult jigsaw puzzle.

I was tempted to send him a nice, tasty carrot.

Do you see how easy it is for a player to help along the element of luck with a little simple psychological trickery? Remember, it could happen to you. Backgammon is tricky, but backgammon players are trickier still. Pitfalls lurk everywhere.

The Safety Pin Strategem

Let's look at another example. My old friend Bob Watts, the unchallenged backgammon champion of the Upper Deer Park Country Club, never tires of saying that the human mind is a complex and devious machine, and who should know better than he? He was taught his lesson by an expert, lovely Ellen Crowther, who knew about rabbits and hats, too.

Ellen is a small, fragile-looking young woman with a vulnerable air and tiny wrists and ankles. She also has enormous innocent blue eyes and a mind like a steel trap. Often, for reasons of her own, she doesn't let the latter quality show. Not right away.

The first time Bob saw Ellen a surge of manly affection swelled his chest. At once he wanted to protect her. Bob is a bachelor and lifelong girl watcher. He is also what is known as a young-man-on-the-way-up. He has a good, logical mind, perfectly equipped for either the higher executive levels of the business world or the split-second decisions that hang on the roll of the dice—and aren't they very much the same?

What is more, Bob is a deep concentrator. He doesn't let trivialities distract him. That is his secret. Once he fixes his attention on the action of a backgammon board, it is almost impossible to draw his mind to other things. The key word there is *almost*.

It was inevitable that Bob and Ellen, two attractive singles and members of the same club, should eventually come face to face over a backgammon board. It happened one rainy evening after a club dance. Nearly everyone had gone home. The game room was empty except for our two friends, and an invitation to play was tendered and accepted.

Instead of sitting at one of the tables, they decided to draw close to the fireplace, in which a log fire was cheerfully crackling. They spread the board between them on the polar bear rug that stretches across the open area in front of the hearth.

Ellen was wearing a clinging white cocktail dress that lovingly revealed her slim, bare arms and shoulders. She sat down gracefully on the rug with her weight slightly forward, toward Bob, and her feet tucked under her. Bob thought she looked absolutely terrific.

They were playing for moderate stakes, and up to the final crucial game, the play was about even. Although Bob was as skillful as always, Ellen had enjoyed a run of luck with the dice. However, thanks to the doubling cube, a considerable amount of cash was riding on that last game. Not a huge amount, mind you, but more, Bob knew, than Ellen could really afford on her salary as a junior public relations executive in a metropolitan department store.

It was at the beginning of this fateful game that she pulled the Safety Pin Stratagem on him.

The Safety Pin Stratagem is a low, dirty trick known to many women who use it against unsuspecting males with great success. It always works on your lifelong devoted girl watcher. It goes like this.

As the game began and Bob picked up the dice cup for his first roll, Ellen suddenly emitted a tiny squeal of dismay.

"Oops!" she squeaked. "There goes my darned safety pin!"

Bob raised his eyebrows solicitously.

"Anything wrong?" he asked.

"Never mind! It's none of your business!"

"But you sounded as though something happened."

Ellen looked shyly down at the board. "Well, if you *must* know," she said, "I just felt my safety pin pop. I think it broke."

Bob couldn't resist. His curiosity was thoroughly aroused. "What safety pin?" he asked.

Believe it or not, Ellen blushed and gave a small giggle.

"You just pay attention to the game," she said in an embarrassed voice.

"Look here," Bob said gallantly, "would you like to go out to the ladies' room and fix it or get another one or something? We can stop playing for a few minutes."

"And break my run of luck? Forget it! Not on your life— I'm in a winning streak! I'll just have to take the risk."

Take the risk!

Bob's razor-sharp brain, often compared to a surgeon's scalpel, went into action. Ellen's dress was charming but skimpy. There was no safety pin visible from where he sat. Therefore, he reasoned, it must be somewhere that was *not* visible. Secondly, Ellen's blush, her giggle, and above all, her use of the word *risk* implied a pin of some importance, one whose malfunction its owner regarded as capable of causing a disastrous situation to arise. How many pinnable items are there in a woman's inner or outer coverings that a nice girl won't talk about? Not many. Bob began to count them in his mind.

Moreover, if Ellen, a modern, liberated young person with no Victorian hangups, was too shy to discuss with a male the location of said pin or what unmentionable items it held precariously and insecurely together, it must be. . . . Here his imagination failed him. It was too much for Bob. From that moment on, his concentration was irretrievably shattered.

For the rest of the game, he paid very little attention to the board, moving his men carelessly from place to place, almost without seeing them. His eyes darted furtively over the surface of Ellen's dress, probing, inspecting, wondering. Ellen, of course, played a magnificent game. She kept him in a constant state of uncertainty.

Every time his eyes left her person and he showed signs of regaining his interest in the game, she uttered a small birdlike chirp of panic, shifting and wriggling in her place, drawing his attention back to her like a magnet.

"Oh oh!" she would warble in accents of despair as he was considering a critical move.

The results were predictable. Wasting double aces to hit her blot on his five point, Bob missed two valuable points at her five and seven. Ellen won hands down, picking up a sum that contributed nicely to her forthcoming vacation at the Club Mediteranée in Martinique, where she had a marvelous time.

Although he lost the game and the money, Bob felt he'd gained an amusing anecdote. He periodically entertained his friends with the story of "the time Ellen Crowther nearly lost her . . ." (his imagination placed the errant fastener here or there, wherever he thought it might most amuse a particular audience).

The incident became part of his personal legend until one evening when he found himself playing a critical game with pretty Grace Harrington. As Bob was preparing to roll the dice, she let out an agonized squeak.

"Oops!" she wailed. "There goes my darned safety pin!"

Bob says it was as though someone had suddenly raised a dusty curtain and flooded a dark room with light.

Bob's experience was a valuable one, and of course, he could afford it, which isn't always the case in experiences of this sort. What is more, he not only learned a lesson but he also made two new friends, both of them lovely to look at. That, too, isn't always the case.

More Rabbits

In twentieth-century America and, for that matter, in most places in the civilized world, there are many backgammon-playing types. Players come in all sizes, shapes, and varieties.

Clearly, the most difficult to outwit are the ones with no wit at all, because those players have no strategy to be turned against them. They chatter endlessly, moving the men in aimless patterns, now offensive, now defensive, with no recourse to logic. For him or her, the game exists only as a way to fill the gaps in an inane and superfluous conversation. A serious player, matched against such a nincompoop, will be courting a nervous breakdown or a series of mini-strokes in no time at all.

It is easy to spot these menaces in advance and just as easy to avoid getting involved with them—if you know what to look for. All you have to do is stand silently for a few minutes in a crowded room. If you realize after a short time that although many people are talking, you can hear only one voice distinctly, that's the one to avoid. Does that voice sound as though its owner is functioning at 45 rpm when 33⅓ would be more appropriate? On guard! Avoid that person like the plague, and, above all, do not allow yourself to be maneuvered into facing him or her across a backgammon board.

Of course, even when exercising the utmost caution, you may find it unavoidable to play with such a creature, perhaps the cousin or brother-in-law of an important customer or business colleague. When that happens to me, I concentrate hard, playing in dead earnest, making every move count.

As the shrill, irritating voice bombards my senses, I nod sagely, indicating agreement. By a kind of autohypnosis, I can disassemble the words, removing their meaning, if any, and transpose them into a kind of verbal Muzak, an accompaniment to the game like the music you hear in elevators and apartment-house lobbies.

In this way, for example, a phrase such as *"So-I-said-to-him-what-do-you-mean-turning-left-without-signalling-where-did-you-learn-to-drive-a-taxicab-what-do-you.think-that-little-gadget-on-the-side-of-the-steering-wheel-is-for-Buster,"* becomes for my trained ear, *"Dum-de-de-dum-dum-DUM-DUM-de-de-de-dah-dah-DAH-de-de-DUM."* Quite a pleasant melody when you get used to it. In a neo-classical kind of way.

Since this sort of player never pays much attention to what is happening on the board, it is particularly easy to get him or her to accept your doubles or even to slip in a power cube if you have one. I've been known to double in the course of a particularly windy anecdote, just before the arrival of the punch line. All you have to do is keep your opponent talking. You can do it with feeder terms, such as "You said it!" or "How *about* that!" A low whistle is sometimes useful, as is a throaty chuckle of appreciation accompanied by an incredulous headshake.

These small encouragements will bring the pest to new heights of rhetoric, which you can nurse along until the game shifts in your favor. Then, when your opponent has accepted the final double and you are ready to go in for the kill, you can cut off the sound track with a few well-chosen words.

An especially effective phrase is, "Shut up and roll!"

Such a statement will have a dual effect: First, it will turn off the noise; second, it will cause your enemy to play recklessly, out of sheer pique, to show you up.

You might point out, after you have pocketed the stakes, that the Chinese have an ancient proverb to the effect that the costliest organ in the human body is the mouth. Maybe you'll get through to him.

And then again, maybe you won't.

3
Suffer Little Children

Children are wonderful. Give them a little love, John Ruskin said, and you'll get a great deal back. They can be a source of great satisfaction and terribly amusing. If the little creatures become tedious, they can be packed off to bed, which is more than can be said for a great many adults.

If there is one activity that children adore, it is playing games. They play hard, even desperately, with a powerful will to win. A competitive game will keep them quiet for hours. Unfortunately, there are few games an adult can share with a nine- or ten-year-old. Checkers is one, since the number of logical decisions is limited compared with similar games such as chess. Bingo, which is one-hundred-percent luck, is another. Youngsters also bear up well against their elders at casino, Monopoly, and some forms of rummy.

It is not unusual for a bright child to learn how to play backgammon well. The strong element of luck in the game helps balance the generation gap. An adult can often enjoy a rattling good prebedtime match with a smart subteen, but don't expect to win every time! Don't imagine when you gaze into those innocent baby-blue eyes that the little darling is a pushover. Remember the rugged will to conquer, the need to see the grown-up knocked off his or her pedestal. In order to enjoy that ultimate thrill, they will often use their diminutive size and their young vulnerability (though I hate to say it) in an underhanded way.

What I mean is, they cheat.

If you think I'm stretching the truth, remember what happened to Morgan Phillips, who fell victim to the Mendacious Midget Artifice. Morgan's adventure ended up for the best, but how many of us are as lucky?

The Mendacious Midget Artifice

The best of players must one day come unglued. Stars tumble; champions bite the dust. No one is infallible, and defeat comes at the most unexpected times and in the most unexpected places. It's the old Samson syndrome. Look at what happened to Goliath. Or, better yet, look at what happened to Morgan Phillips.

Morgan was a champion. Backgammon was his game, and he had a trophy to prove his supremacy. In a glass-fronted case in his hallway sat a small silver cup neatly engraved with his name and a few significant particulars: the symbol of the North Beach Country Club and the date of the final match of that organization's annual Masters Backgammon Tournament.

Morgan was a tournament-class player. Over the years he had honed his backgammon skills and sensibilities to a razor's edge. His pace was formidable. He would bring the cup down with a quick, graceful swoop, expelling the dice neatly to the rim of the board but no further. In the twinkling of an eye, it was *click-click*, *zip-zip*, a man here, a man there, and on to the next roll. Speed was his trademark. The spectators loved him. He had style.

He was also a perfectionist, and rightly so, since, as a backgammon player, he was very close to being perfect. He made no secret of this fact. Just the opposite. He was glad to discourse on it at any opportunity. To Morgan's mind, perfection, especially his own, was something to be admired, and why not share it with the world at large?

Morgan's nonpareil qualities extended beyond the limits of the backgammon board into other facets of his life. He was unmarried, for what wife could survive in such a flawless, rarified atmosphere? A normal girl thrust into his life style would probably shrivel like a sensitive plant that has had too much sun. Besides, Morgan suspected that women are prone to doing revolting things, such as moving one's ashtrays about and making dents in one's sofa cushions when they sit down. Better not to take the risk.

No speck of dust ever sullied the gleaming, polished surfaces that graced the furnishings of his apartment. His lordly Mercedes glided soundlessly through fashionable neighborhoods, its valves innocent of carbon. His well-cut trousers revealed no evidence that he ever sat, kneeled, stooped, or even walked. You could shave with their knifelike creases if you liked, using his glistening Lobb shoes for a mirror.

Such a man was Morgan Phillips, but alas, as so frequently happens to such men (even Achilles had a foot condition), there was a fly struggling fiercely in the balmy ointment of his life. One adamant rebellious pea lurked under the twenty-three mattresses that cushioned his existence, bruising his sensitive hide.

Morgan had relatives.

From the earliest days of his childhood, Morgan had always been appalled by his kinfolk, who were, let's face it, not a bit like him. How was it possible, he had always wondered, for a man of his quality to be born into a family made up of commonplace churls like them?

For it must be faced that Morgan's relations were earthy, ordinary plain folks such as live in bungalow suburbs, eat in their shirt sleeves, bowl on Wednesday nights, watch ball games on television, drink beer from the can, and wear pink plastic curlers in their hair. They purchased their art collection at Woolworth's, read the *Reader's Digest,* fantasized with Harold Robbins and Irving Wallace, and never played backgammon.

Morgan pretended they didn't exist. He never thought about them unless it was absolutely necessary, and on those rare occasions when thinking about them was unavoidable, he thought about them with fastidious distaste.

But the fact is, they did exist. And as Morgan himself would be the first to tell you, families, like boils, have a tendency to appear out of nowhere at the most inconvenient times.

One lovely spring morning Morgan was enjoying breakfast on his sun-washed terrace. Below him the East River meandered toward the Bronx, bearing on its bosom a picturesque barge, a few tugs, and a Circle Line sight-seeing boat, which, at that very moment (Morgan was positive), was bearing a crowd of admiring vulgarians instructed by their guide to raise their eyes and note the location of the Great Man's (his) residence. Birds were singing, the first roses were in bloom, and the opening day of the year's North Beach Country Club Tournament (the Mixed Singles Backgammon Open) was scheduled for after lunch.

Life could not have been sweeter. He tossed a handful of croissant crumbs to a hungry sparrow and relaxed in his chair, humming a few bars of "The Death of Manolete." It promised to be a perfectly splendid day.

At that moment the telephone rang. With no thoughts of

ominous prospects ahead, he spoke a melodious greeting into the cream-colored mouthpiece, but as the speaker identified herself, his mouth dropped open. His eyes bulged. Beads of perspiration appeared on his smooth brow. His breakfast turned to lead in his stomach. His hand shook.

The voice that answered him was that of his sister Ethel.

Morgan allowed an exclamation of dismay to escape him—a sort of unaspirated "ha," like the hiss of a punctured bicycle tire. When Ethel called, it usually meant bad news. This call was no exception to the rule. Her voice rattled in his ear like a Texas sidewinder, without pausing for breath.

"Aunt Dora?" he said, a small smile beginning to break through the thundercloud of his frown. "Dead?"

"Yesterday," Ethel said. "Poor soul. She was under the knife for hours. A tumor the size of a cantaloupe. She died in her sleep in the intensive-care recovery room. The doctor said she probably didn't feel any pain at all."

"Too bad," Morgan muttered. "I'll send flowers. Better still, I'll make a donation in her name to the National Backgammon Foundation."

But that was by no means that. The telephone ignored his interruption and chattered on like a living thing. As Ethel's message got through to him, his face twisted in a grimace of pain and he turned deadly pale under his Antigua tan. His expression resembled that worn by John Barrymore in the mad scene of *A Bill of Divorcement*, when he fancied that a shapeless black mass was rising out of the floor to engulf him. Speechless, he hung up the telephone with a trembling hand.

In brief, Ethel's message was this. She and Bert, her husband, were planning to fly to Wisconsin to stage-manage Aunt Dora's last rites. This left their nine-year-old son, Bernie, unattended, his regular sitter being stricken with measles. To offset this family crisis, Morgan was required to spend the night at their place to attend to Bernie's needs and keep him out of trouble. Ethel and Bert would return the following day.

"*Aaagggh!*" said Morgan to the now-silent telephone, sitting in its cradle unaware of the harm it had done.

The celebrated film director Federico Fellini would have been delighted with the scene that unfolded in the suburban living room of the absent Bert and Ethel Krumbauer on the following evening. On one side of the room, in a sagging armchair covered with faded rose-patterned chintz, sat Morgan, dressed in a fawn-colored lightweight tweed jacket and pale grey flannel slacks, his feet in fringe-flapped mocha suede loafers. On the other side sat Bernie, small, fattish, and bespectacled, in shapeless corduroy jeans, Adidas sneakers, and a *National Lampoon* T-shirt. His nose was running. Morgan, having nervously ascertained that Bernie did not have a bad cold, dared not imagine what the state of the child's nostrils would be if he *did* have a cold.

"Well!" said Morgan, clearing his throat.

Bernie regarded him with a frigid, unwinking stare.

"Well! . . . uh . . . fella . . . I guess you'd like to read a comic book now or watch some good old sci-fi on the television." He looked at Bernie hopefully.

"No, I wouldn't."

There was a silence. Morgan shuddered slightly, a reaction to the frozen pizza he had been forced to share with his charge for dinner.

"Well, what *would* you like to do?" Morgan asked, dreading the answer.

"I wanna play backgammon."

Backgammon!

For a moment, Morgan was appalled by the outright

sacrilege of it. Backgammon played by this grubby urchin, and played, moreover, under a lamp that represented a Venetian gondolier, dressed for some reason in a gold bolero jacket and a fancy turban? Backgammon, in a room with a three-dimensional plaster portrait of the late General Douglas MacArthur propped up on the combination fake fireplace and stereo?

Then, slowly, the basic goodness of Morgan's nature began to ooze through. After all, Bernie was his flesh-and-blood nephew. Maybe, with a little coaching and a great deal of patience, a kindly uncle might lead the kid through the first fumbling steps that would set him on the road to becoming another Morgan Phillips. Someday, perhaps, the boy might lift up the torch when an aged (but still attractive) Morgan was ready to lay it down. Miracles do happen. Even if the kid turned out to be as impossible as he looked, at least he, Morgan, could teach him the rudiments of the game. Just a few pointers, so he could lord it over his little classmates. Besides, he didn't seem to have much choice in the matter.

"All right," Morgan said.

"I'll get the board," Bernie said.

In a trice Bernie vanished into the noisome dark that blanketed the bedroom area of the house and returned with a gray, limp object folded over his arm. To Morgan's disgust, he realized at once that it was one of those oversized terrycloth beach towels with backgammon markings which are supposedly amusing for playing on the sand.

"This is the board?" he asked, hoping it wasn't.

"Yeah. Just move your foot a little and I'll put it down here on the floor."

Suiting the action to the word, Bernie spread the towel on the ancient flokati rug in whose matted nap Morgan observed for the first time: dog hairs, chewing gum, fuzz-covered hard candies, peanut butter stains, and something crumbly that might at one time have been either kitty litter or a chocolate chip cookie.

"Come on," Bernie said, "sit down."

"On the floor?"

"Where else? You can't reach the men from up there."

Carefully plucking up his trousers at the knee, Morgan lowered himself gingerly. He drew a deep breath. Bernie produced a shoe box full of oddly-assorted objects and began to distribute them about the towel.

"What in God's name are those?"

"Those are the *men*, stupid."

"These are the men?"

"Well, some of them got lost or something, and we had to put these in."

"A marble?"

Bernie ignored the question and laid out the "men" carefully. With an exclamation of impatience, Morgan dislodged an ancient marshmallow from the heel of his shoe.

"All right," he said firmly. "Roll the dice."

Bernie took a Campbell's soup can out of the shoebox and placed it between them. It proved to be full of slips of paper.

"What now, for heaven's sake? Where are the dice?"

"My mother won't let me play with real dice. She says it doesn't look nice for a nine-year-old. She says I'll take them to school and get in trouble."

"So how are we supposed to play backgammon without dice?"

Bernie drew a well-thumbed slip of paper out of the can. On it were drawn in a childish hand two uneven squares, one containing three dots and the other four.

"A three and four," he said. Each of the slips in the can portrayed a possible combination of two dice. There were thirty-six slips in all.

"Good God!" Morgan said, fascinated in spite of himself. He reached in and pulled out double threes.

"I go first," Bernie said, producing a battered piggy bank from beneath the sofa. From it he extracted a flaccid dollar bill, which he laid at the edge of the board. The game was on.

No doubt about it, Morgan told me later in the game room of the club, the kid knew how to play. He was, Morgan could see, an advocate of the careful back game, leaving blots for his uncle to hit, preferring to build up a formidable home board. Morgan approved of his nephew's tactics, being rather good at back games himself. However, he had no intention of letting Bernie win. Losing his dollar, Morgan reasoned, would be a valuable lesson for the boy.

"Aha!" he cried triumphantly, pouncing on one of Bernie's strategically placed blots and sending it to the bar.

"Aha yourself! That's not my man. It's yours."

"The marble is *yours!* It's red, which means it's one of the blacks."

"Red is white, not black."

"Now see here! It's nothing of the kind!"

"The Alka-Seltzer tablet is white, so it's white. The Lindsay button is brown, so it's black. But the marble is red, so it's white."

Morgan's head was spinning. "So how come," he asked, "the peppermint is black if the marble is white? They're both red."

"The peppermint is red and white *striped*, stupid. Striped is always black."

A bead of perspiration coursed down Morgan's forehead. Bernie threw two doubles in a row and bore home his last

"The Alka-Seltzer tablet is white, the Lindsay button is black, the peppermint is white, the marble is black, the chocolate chip cookie. . . ."

men, winning the game. He leaned over, picked up Morgan's dollar and began to set up a new game.

By nine o'clock, the kid's irrevocable bedtime, Morgan had lost seven dollars and had not won a single game. Bernie scampered off to his bedroom whistling a shrill off-key version of the "Colonel Bogey March," leaving his stricken uncle stretched amid the rubble on the floor, a broken and defeated man.

Morgan struggled to his feet and mopped his brow. Not only had he missed the opening day of his club's most important tournament of the year, but now he had suffered this humiliation at the hands of a child of nine! He sank into the armchair, which groaned in protest. Perhaps the best thing would be to go to bed.

He rose and began to turn off the lamps. As he was moving toward the door, his foot struck the soup can, and the "dice" spilled out onto the carpet. With a sigh of annoyance he knelt and began to pick them up.

"So that was how he did it," I said at the club next day, unable to hold back a grin. Morgan and I were enjoying a late afternoon martini near the swimming pool. "The kid was cheating all the time, was he?"

"Indeed he was," Morgan said, with perhaps a tiny bit of pride shining through his disapproval. "But this morning at breakfast I was ready for him. I stripped him to the bone. Absolutely took the little bandit to the cleaners."

He opened an ostrich-hide attaché case and took out a battered piggy bank, three limp one-dollar bills, an assortment of baseball cards, a cap pistol, and a Swiss Army knife with one broken blade.

"Wow! You really broke the bank."

"I certainly did. When I picked up those slips of paper and found that there were only thirty-one of them instead of thirty-six, I knew exactly what he was up to. It didn't matter which five were missing as far as winning the game went, but if only one player knew which ones were not there, it gave him a tremendous advantage over his opponent. He could calculate my chances of getting a roll I needed. When he doubled, he was practically betting on a sure thing."

"I wondered about those slips. It seemed to me that it would have been simpler to have only twelve slips showing the numbers one through six twice, instead of making all thirty-six combinations. You'd have the same effect with a lot less work."

"I thought that, too, but then I said to myself, he's only a little boy."

"Some little boy!"

"So I simply took his crayon, which was lying on the floor with the rest of the rubble, and drew in the missing "dice" in an excellent approximation, if I do say so myself, of his own style. Then I removed five slips, but not the ones he thought were missing."

"And after breakfast?"

"I suggested a game. He snapped up the bait and that was that."

"Very clever," I said. "Another martini?"

"No, thanks, I want to stop in the club secretary's office before closing time."

"Going to cash a check?"

"No. I'm putting Bernie up for membership on his twenty-first birthday."

If I'm still around when Bernie reaches his majority, I'll be interested in seeing how he makes out. For those who would like a duplicate of the boy's board, one need only to contact Morgan Phillips, in care of the Club Secretary. He and Bernie sell them for $25.00 apiece. They make wonderful Christmas gifts.

More Backgammon Brats

You see what children are capable of? And Bernie is not unique. Nor do little boys have a monopoly on sharp practices in the backgammon area. Little girls are just as bad. My old friend Phil Porter, for example, who sometimes carries his board to the shores of the Pacific Ocean near San Francisco, once found himself sitting opposite a dainty, golden-haired moppet on a park bench. The little creature watched him moving the men about and suggested a game. With a smile, Phil acquiesced and set out the men in their positions.

The child, whose name she informed Phil was Emily, looked like a small angel in a painting. She obviously knew her stuff and played well, but in the long run experience told, and Phil began to win. With this, her radiant smile vanished and the game took on a new character. Emily, who was barely ten, suddenly and unaccountably burst into tears every time he sent one of her men to the bar. This necessitated many pauses in the game for the purpose of reassuring her and drying her streaming eyes. A number of nursemaids turned and frowned at Phil, and a suspicious-looking policeman ambled over to stand in the vicinity of their bench. Phil grinned at them nervously, but it was no use. There was only one course open to him. He stopped hitting blots and in due course lost the game and two others. The kid took him for three dollars, a hot dog, and a box of Cracker Jack.

The end result was a conditioned reflex that ruined Phil's game for months. Evey time he had an opportunity to hit an adversary's blot, he would break out in a cold sweat and make a different move.

Jim Riordan of the Bridgehampton club had a similar experience with an eight-year-old neighbor, a manly little fellow reminiscent of the illustrations in *Winnie the Pooh*. With such a face, Jim reasoned, the boy could only grow up to a life of truth and beauty or possibly a partnership in a good brokerage house. As for cheating at backgammon . . . perish the thought! Since the child was so young, Jim played down to him, helping him along, but even so, as the game progressed, he found himself on the brink of winning a gammon on which rested a stake of three Matchbook racing cars and a plastic water pistol.

As Jim shook the dice cup, the silence was broken by a hideous, rasping, retching sound. It could mean only one thing.

The child had swallowed his jawbreaker!

Jim leaped up, shouting for someone to get a doctor. He turned the boy upside down and pounded him on the back. With great relief he heard the retching stop and saw the boy's eyelids flutter open. He was all right. The doctor would not be necessary. The hard candy had gone past the critical area into the child's stomach, where it would melt and be digested.

"It's your roll," the little fellow croaked hoarsely, but Jim firmly refused to continue the game. He put the stake back into the child's pocket and added his own, a shiny new Kennedy half-dollar.

"No more playing for you, young man," he said. "I concede. You'd better run along home."

Which is exactly what the little chap did, pulling from his pocket, as soon as he was out of sight, a large and somewhat lint-speckled jawbreaker, which he returned to its former place in his mouth.

You see what can happen when you let your guard down

even for a minute? But what can one do about children who cheat at backgammon? It would appear at first glance that they hold all the weapons. How can one beat them at their own game?

Simple! My neighbor Willard Parsons has never lost to a child in twenty-five years of play. How does Willard do it? "Nothing to it," Will says. As soon as he's set up the board and handed the dice cup to his tiny opponent to roll for first play, he stands up and very slowly and meaningfully removes his belt, taking plenty of time with each loop. He lays the belt down beside the board. Then he reaches into his jacket pocket and pulls out a fine old ebony hair brush, which he places next to the belt.

"Works like a charm," Will says. He hasn't yet been flummoxed by a ten-year-old, male or female. And, best of all, it's educational. Who knows but that someday one of his opponents may grow up to be president, thanks to Will's little lesson.

4
Never Laugh at a Stand-up Karmic

It should certainly come as no surprise to anyone that there is a mystical quality about backgammon. Devotees of the game are always pointing out that the dice appear to roll into patterns and combinations that seem to be guided or preordained by some divine or occult force. Whether this is simply an amalgam of plain dumb luck and Murphy's Law* or whether there is actually someone or something up there calling the shots, philosophers never have been able to decide.

It does seem unlikely that busy and all-powerful deities, like Jehovah, Allah, Buddha, or even good old Satan, would take time out from what must be overwhelmingly full schedules in order to peer over one's shoulder and set up a

---

*The most complete version of Murphy's Law is quoted in Charles Issawi's *Issawi's Laws of Social Motion* (Hawthorn, 1973).

1. Anything that can go wrong will go wrong.

2. If there is a possibility of more than one thing going wrong, the thing that will go wrong will be the one that will do the most damage.

3. Left to themselves, things always go from bad to worse.

4. Nature always sides with the hidden flaw.

5. If it appears that everything is going right, you are probably unaware of all that is happening.

gammon with the doubling cube standing at thirty-two. I prefer to think that backgammon luck is controlled according to the Greek system, which supplied a different god for every occasion, all of whom had time to pop down for quick partisan interference in mortal matters. After all, the Greeks knew about backgammon and so did the Romans. It's not impossible that the game had its own god.

Master Plans

A man much interested in mystical matters was Fred Burnham. In his college years, Fred had dabbled in (in rapid succession) the works of Dr. Coué, Aleister Crowley and Madame Blavatsky, Sufi with a bit of Yoga and TM on the side, Bahai, the Q'abbalah, and the worship of Kali. For a while, he had toyed with the idea of joining the Hari Krishnas, but the managing partner of the Wall Street brokerage house that employed him talked him out of it. He explained to Fred that the company might accept a shaven head but would definitely draw the line at his appearing in a saffron nightgown and sandals.

At the office Fred was a good, sound, hard-working fellow. It was only after hours that he delved into esoterica. On his vacations, when he felt (and quite correctly) that his time was exclusively his own, he pursued his special interests with enthusiasm.

Thus it came to pass that a recent July found him clad in khaki shorts and rubber-soled hiking shoes, bearing a backpack that contained a few balls of glutinous rice and a Tibetan prayer wheel, struggling up a small mountain in Sullivan County toward the residence of the noted Zen master, T'ang.

Master T'ang (who, in an earlier karma had been one

Mort Greiber, assistant professor of accounting at LaGuardia Community College) lived in a small, handsome saltbox not far from Ellenville. There he subsisted on the bounty of his disciples and did a great deal of meditating.

After much climbing and several pauses to ask directions, Fred arrived at last at the master's gate, where he encountered the great man's chief disciple, Debbie, a pretty young woman with large hazel eyes and long yellow hair. She was wearing a plain white cheesecloth tunic a little too small for her in places. Fred examined her with approval.

Debbie's job as number-one disciple was to keep house for Master T'ang and prepare his simple meals. She also, when necessary, rubbed his back with a mitten made of cat fur to ward off rheumatism. As soon as she spotted Fred coming in the gate, she gave him a welcoming smile.

"Many journey to sit at the master's feet and partake of his wisdom, but even those who arrive do not always reach him," she said.

"Never a truer word was spoken," Fred agreed. "I'd like to dip into some of that renowned wisdom, if convenient, with an eye to self-improvement. Is the master in?"

"He is traveling," Debbie said.

Fred's face fell. "Well, maybe I can come another time," he said.

"Not traveling in the corporeal sense," Debbie explained. "He is traveling in the astral plane. At four o'clock he returns to earth to partake of his simple repast, a tongue sandwich on sour rye with Hellman's prepared by my unworthy hands."

Fred looked at the unworthy hands, which were small and white with long tapering fingers and beautifully shaped rosy nails.

"You mean he eats meat?" he asked in some surprise.

"He does not *eat* meat in the sense that the uninitiated

would eat meat—for foolish physical gratification. He absorbs the *essence* of meat by taking it into his body through the orifice of the mouth."

"So *every* afternoon at four o'clock he comes to earth to eat a tongue sandwich?"

"Sometimes a ham and cheese with cole slaw. And to enjoy his favorite pastime." She looked modestly down at her pretty toes peeping out of her little thong sandals.

"His favorite pastime?" Fred asked nervously, following her gaze downward.

"A game of backgammon."

"Ah. The master plays backgammon?"

"How often does the answer to the secret of destiny lie in the cast of the die?"

"Oh yes," said Fred. "How very, very often."

At that moment, their conversation was interrupted by the sound of a nose being vigorously blown inside the house, and the creaking of floorboards heralded the master's return to this planet from the astral plane.

"Damn!" Debbie said, looking nervously at the house. "I'd better get my butt out to the kitchen. See you later." She vanished rapidly around the side of the building.

As Debbie's little cheesecloth tunic whipped out of sight, the master himself appeared on the porch, yawning widely and blinking like an owl in the afternoon sunlight. He spotted Fred standing in the yard and raised his eyebrows.

Master T'ang was clad in an Indian blanket bathrobe tied loosely at the waist with a length of clothesline. His pepper-and-salt bearded face was wrinkled and brown like a walnut shell. Around his balding skull was a wiry fringe of grayish hair. His eyes were bright and shrewd. He examined Fred closely, from hiking shoes to tennis hat with transparent green plastic insert.

"Welcome, traveler from a far distance," he said.

"Thank you," Fred replied politely, "and welcome home to you, too."

"To me?"

"Yes. From the astral plane, I mean."

"Oh that. Well, sit down." Master T'ang indicated with a gesture a straw mat on the porch. He himself sat down in a wicker rocking chair.

"Master," Fred said in a voice of deep sincerity, "I have come to catch the pearls of wisdom that drop from your venerable lips."

The master cocked his head to one side like a stork and regarded Fred appraisingly. Then he spoke.

"Under the Shen Yan Bridge there are many waters," he said.

Fred thought about that for a minute. Then he asked, "Master, what does that mean?"

"The meaning is within the words as the kernel is within the nut. But the difficult outer shell can be cracked to release the meat within. It is necessary only to find the Way. When you find it, it will appear to you suddenly as in a blinding flash of light. But it may take much time. Perhaps years."

"Years?"

"The teacher offers the lesson. If the student cannot find the meaning, the lesson is worthless."

"I see," said Fred, scribbling in his notebook.

At that moment Debbie reappeared carrying a dish with the master's simple repast, three cans of Dr. Pepper, and a flat box. She placed them on a small table near the master's right hand, taking one can for herself and offering a second to Fred. Then she sat down on the mat beside him, tucking her feet under her in the Japanese fashion. Fred waited patiently, notebook in hand, until the master had finished his sandwich and wiped his beard with a paper napkin. Master T'ang belched softly and picked up his Dr. Pepper.

"The uneaten tongue was in the sandwich," he said, "as the small unused womb lies in the body of the female child. Now the sandwich is in my own body as the child lies in the womb of the mother."

"Amen," Fred said, nodding his head with understanding.

"Yet soon all will be dust. Would you like to play a game of backgammon?"

The wooden box Debbie had brought proved, indeed, to be a backgammon set, and in no time at all she had laid out the men and handed each of them a dice cup. She sat back and arranged her legs in the lotus position. Fred put on his glasses.

"Master T'ang plays Zen backgammon," Debbie said, by way of explanation.

Fred had never heard of Zen backgammon, but he had read about Zen archery and Zen motorcycle maintenance. That the master should play Zen backgammon seemed only logical. He prepared himself for a mystical experience. Knowing he was an expert player, he was sure he could pick up the rules for this particular variety as he went along.

As the first game progressed, it became obvious to Fred that, in spite of the master's ancient wisdom, he, Fred, was the better player. Without too much effort he slid easily into a gammon and pocketed the small stake that the master had insisted on betting on the outcome—to give the ancients in the Outer Perimeter a chance to participate in the game. Waving away Fred's apology, Master T'ang smiled inscrutably.

"The coins of earth are as grains of desert sand in the wind," he said kindly. "They can cause small irritation or the erosion of mighty mountains."

"How true," Fred said.

Up to this point, Fred had noted no discernable difference between Zen backgammon and the ordinary variety. But he had gathered enough pearls from the lips of the master to realize that if there were a difference, it would come to him in time (perhaps years), as in a flash of light.

As the games continued, the stakes rose to formidable heights. Fred looked nervously at the neat but certainly not ostentatious house with its tidy little garden. Could Master T'ang afford to lose so much? After all, he, Fred, was a guest in the master's house, or at least on the master's porch.

He looked at the board. Master T'ang had a solid four-point board, as well as having his bar point covered. The master's dice cup rattled ferociously, while Fred took a long, nonchalant pull on his Dr. Pepper.

This is how the board looked:

MASTER T'ANG

OUTER BOARD   HOME BOARD

MASTER
T'ANG'S
ROLL

OUTER BOARD   HOME BOARD

FRED

The master rolled a two and three. Bringing his man in from the bar, he hit Fred's five point blot, but then proceeded to move three more fives, hitting Fred's other blot in the process. Fred stared at his two men sitting disconsolately on the bar, then up at Master T'ang.

"Uh . . . pardon me, master," Fred said politely. "You rolled a two and a three, not double fives. You moved your men as though you had rolled double fives," he explained.

"A miracle! A Zen miracle!" Debbie whispered reverently.

"A what?"

"A Zen miracle. Don't you understand? Think of the tomato plant."

"What tomato plant?"

"The uninitiated think that if a tomato plant blossomed with roses or bananas it would be a miracle. But the devotees of Zen are wiser. Because of the random quality of life, such a random blooming would be quite normal. But if only tomatoes grow on the same vine, that is the antithesis of randomness and thus becomes a miracle."

"But what does that have to do with Master T'ang rolling a two and a three and moving his men as though he had rolled double fives?"

"In rolling the dice, the random result is the norm. But if the pieces on the board are moved *outside* the limited restrictions of numerical accident or printed numbers, that is a manifestation of Zen force," the master explained.

"The master has performed a miracle before our eyes," Debbie whispered in awe. "Oh how fortunate we are."

Master T'ang gave Fred a benign smile and nodded sagely.

"Now wait a minute . . ." Fred began, but Master T'ang placed his fingers on Fred's lips, silencing him.

"It could take years," he said gently, lifting the dice cup and passing it to Fred. "Your turn."

"The meaning is within the words as the kernel is within the nut. But the difficult outer shell may be cracked to release the meat within. It is necessary only to find The Way. Your move."

A run of extremely good luck made Fred feel somewhat calmer as the game continued, and he pulled ahead again. With only two men left, he was jubilant as he eyed Master T'ang's remaining four. But it was the master's turn to throw and Fred was wary. Closing his eyes and moving his lips, presumably in prayer, the master threw. The dice came up double six. Grinning with pleasure, he pocketed the stakes, which by this time had reached check and BankAmericard proportions, rose to his sandaled feet, and bowed to Fred.

"But you rolled double six and you *moved* double six," Fred cried, jumping up. "You followed the random quality of the dice this time but not before. Why no Zen miracle this time?"

"Two monks were walking down a country lane," the master said, putting his hand on Fred's head. "They came to a stream swollen with spring floods. At the edge of the stream stood a beautiful maiden. She was weeping because the muddy current was too strong for her to cross the stream. The first monk greeted her and then he lifted her in his arms. He waded across the stream and set her down on the far side."

"Yes, master," Fred said, "but. . . ."

"That night, the monks rested at a monastery. When they had eaten and retired for the night, the second monk spoke in accusation. 'How could you have broken our vows?' he asked his companion. 'You know we are forbidden to speak to women, yet you not only spoke to the girl but lifted her in your arms as well!' "

"Yes, but listen, Master T'ang . . .," Fred began.

"The first monk replied, 'My brother, I put the girl down on the opposite side of the stream. Do you still carry her with you?' "

With a smile of infinite gentleness, Master T'ang bowed to Fred and entered his small house, closing the door behind him, leaving Fred sputtering with unanswered questions. Debbie began to put the backgammon pieces back into the box.

"Now look here!" Fred began.

"The master's parable was meant to initiate you into the lowest entry levels of the ancient wisdom," Debbie explained, rising to her feet and smoothing the skirt of her tunic. "The story of the two monks illustrates the transitory quality of past and future. Only the present has real existence."

"In other words, what Master T'ang did earlier has no bearing at all on what he did later or on what he might decide to do tomorrow?"

"You got it."

"But how can you play a game that way?" Fred said. "With no past or future you can't have any rules, and you can't play any game without rules. It doesn't matter what number comes up on the dice, because you can interpret them any way you like, because rules only exist for the instant the dice roll to a stop!"

"It may be years before true understanding comes to you."

And then it came to him, like a blinding flash of light.

A few weeks after the incident, I ran into Fred at the University Club. "So you're into the Hindu sects now," I said over a southside at the bar.

"Yes, I am. They're fascinating. Debbie is learning to play the sitar."

"Debbie? You mean she's come down from Master T'ang's mountaintop?"

"Yes. Poor child. She had nowhere to go, so I'm putting her up at my place. She pays her way, so to speak, by preparing my simple meals and rubbing my back with a mitten made of cat fur. She says it wards off rheumatism."

"Wonderful. I hope you didn't lose too much money to Master T'ang."

"The money is unimportant compared to the wisdom I absorbed. Besides, I popped over to the bank first thing Monday morning and stopped the check."

"But wasn't that a little dishonest? After all, a backgammon debt is a debt of honor."

"Only to the uninitiated. To a Zen master it is quite understandable. You see, Master T'ang went to cash my check in what for him was the present. But the check had by that time been written in my past, so it didn't really exist for either of us."

"He must have been surprised."

"Not very. I sent him a telegram when I got back to the city. It read simply, "I STOPPED THE CHECK. DO YOU STILL CARRY IT WITH YOU?""

"So you did get something out of the master's parable after all."

"I certainly did."

"Well," I said, pushing back my chair and looking at my watch, "nice to have seen you."

Fred looked at me solemnly.

"*Om!*" he said.

The Metaphysical Maneuver

The blending of mystical religious arcana into backgammon only favors the adept who introduces it. Therefore, it is easy to confound these latter-day witch doctors by simply introducing your own. It doesn't matter whether the ritual is false or genuine; if you're the master and he's the novice, he won't know the difference.

The objective of this kind of skulduggery is to minimize the game in relation to the philosophy, as Master T'ang tried so unsuccessfully to do with Fred. If you let your mind wander off the board, perhaps as far as to the astral plane, your opponent is bound to do the same. For example, if your adversary seems to be enjoying an unusual run of good luck, try stopping the game short because "it's time for your meditation"—transcendental or otherwise. Insist on ten minutes of absolute silence. Lie down flat on the floor. Breathe deeply. Or assume the yoga position, which requires that you be upside down with your legs tied in a knot.

If that doesn't break your opponent's lucky streak, nothing will. As a last resort, you might try talking to the dice and the men. Or you might play a record of atonal electronic music for them. Explain that it works with your plants.

The Sham Shrink Shuffle

Harry Morgenstern of Oklahoma City recently wrote me about an opponent who successfully threw him off his game for most of the summer. The hustle she pulled on him is well-known in backgammon circles. It is called The Sham Shrink Shuffle.

No sooner had Harry sat down across the table from this evildoer and begun to roll the dice, than she fixed him with a beady eye and began a complete pyschiatric examination.

"Did you love your mother?" she began.

"Of course I loved my mother! I still do," Harry said, annoyed.

"Then why are you annoyed at my question?"

"I'm not annoyed," Harry said, more annoyed than before.

"Obviously you are. Have I touched a tender point?"

"Roll the dice," Harry said.

"You seem to be more interested in the dice than you are in your mother," she went on. "Do the dice represent something special to you? The dice lying next to the points on the board as they are now, for example. Do you see the points as phallic symbols? Do they threaten you because you feel some inadequacy in that area?"

"Now just one minute, young woman . . .," Harry began, but she ignored him.

"Look at the dice cup. See its long tubular shape and its round, open, gaping mouth? What does *that* suggest to you, Mr. Morgenstern? I declare, your face is quite purple! Do you have a blood pressure problem? Is that why you chose the red side instead of black? Because of its suggestion of blood?"

Harry had had just about enough. By this time, he was so rattled he didn't know where his home board was. He lost the game and the next two. But there is a way to defeat these creatures, Harry says. He figured it out on the way home.

The next time he played against an amateur psychiatrist he was ready. After fielding two or three questions, he said calmly, "I assure you, there is nothing wrong with me. I have been analyzed recently and given a clean bill of health except for one very minor matter."

"What's that?" the pest wanted to know.

"It's nothing really. It only happens when I lose at backgammon. When that last man is born home something happens inside. It's as though I am standing in a long tunnel and a high wind is blowing, screaming, shrieking like some kind of hellish trumpet in my ears so loudly that I can't stand it and I clap my hands over my ears and my hands stick there while my head seems to be shrinking—shrinking down to the size of a pea but my brain remains its usual size so the pressure is unbearable and the pain . . . the pain . . . I think I won't be able to stand it; my brain imploding like a fish suddenly thrust down to a depth miles below its usual habitat and then my body becomes flabby, soft, an evil slimy effluvium gushing from every pore, the stench unbearable and I scream and scream but no sound comes out and I raise my arms but they move in spite of me and I can't control them because they are like animals from some filthy jungle, hairy and vicious, malignant and filled with hatred and I try to hold them back because I know they mean harm—terrible harm—but they are too strong and they grow longer and longer, reaching for my opponent like snakes of some enormous breed and I scream again and then suddenly everything goes black and sometimes I don't wake up for several days and then they tell me what I have done, and . . . ."

Harry says that by the time he reaches that point his opponent has put down the dice cup and is halfway down to the parking lot. He hasn't lost a game to an amateur shrink since that first time.

"Maybe it's unfair," Harry said, "but after all, those rascals shouldn't ought to talk about my mother that way."

5
The Chic Sheikh

In recent years, backgammon has become closely allied with the chic. The game is "in," which is, as we all know, the antithesis of "out," and who in his right mind would want to be "out"?

The in-ness of backgammon has resulted in a number of side effects. There are couturier-designed backgammon costumes. There are bespoke boards inlaid with precious metals or jewels, constructed to the owners' specifications at Swain, Adeney & Briggs of Piccadilly, Asprey's, or Hermes. And, of course, there are backgammon books. Dozens of them.

An especially loathsome side product of backgammon's new face is the Chic Sheikh, so called for easy identification only, since this breed is neither fashionable nor a member of a fine old Arab family. If you're paying attention, you'll hear about one such specimen in a moment. Read carefully. The next victim could be you!

Pompous Circumstances

The *risorgimento* of backgammon came in the early 1970's when a certain Prince Alexis Obolensky launched a high-powered publicity campaign to arouse interest in the game. In no time at all backgammon became highly social, a pastime for "persons of consequence" once again, replacing such faded predecessors as Mah-Jongg and canasta. The upper crust invested heavily in Gucci traveling boards and formed exclusive clubs dedicated more to keeping out undesirables than to the enjoyment of the game itself.

One such club is Chetwode's in midtown New York. Located at an ultrafashionable address, Chetwode's is a masterpiece of deep-pile crimson carpeting and underplayed soft illumination. There is a fine old mahogany bar salvaged whole from some forgotten Cunard liner. For those who wish a brief respite from play, there is a stainless steel dance floor, carefully scratch finished so that it doesn't reflect anything that ought not to be reflected. It has been estimated that if lightning ever struck Chetwode's, half of the *New York Social Register* would be electrocuted. Unless, of course, they were dancing in rubber-soled shoes.

It was at Chetwode's that I renewed my acquaintance with Sam Wentworth. Sam is what is known in certain circles as a scion. A scion is, of course, the same thing as a descendant or more simply a younger member of what is known in the United States as a "good family." Sam isn't the least bit interested in rubbing noses with the important people who congregate at Chetwode's, being sufficiently important himself, and he has no desire to profit from the game, although large sums frequently cross the tables. It is enough for Sam to have a quiet match with a comfortable companion and a moderate stake to add a bit of spice to the play.

It was just such a game in which Sam and I found ourselves engaged one wintry evening in the small game room at Chetwode's. Behind us, but just out of sight, dancers chatted politely and moved to the strains of an old Rodgers and Hart tune. Glasses clinked softly at the bar.

Around us eddied the muted hum that always accompanies good living among the well behaved. The dice clicked; the men moved on and off the board. Suddenly, I saw Sam's mouth tighten in disapproval. His expression was that of a man who has discovered a cockroach swimming feebly in his vichyssoise.

I looked up quickly to see what had disturbed him and observed a florid, heavyset man entering the room. The newcomer wore an obtrusively expensive suit of somewhat extreme cut and handmade Italian shoes festooned with small gold horse brasses. His abundant black hair was plastered down on his head with some overly aromatic pomade, and his pink face was as smooth as an egg, except for a small, pencil-line moustache. He wore a loud, striped silk shirt. On the small finger of his left hand a large diamond ring winked vulgarly in the rosy light of the game-room lamps.

Probably the most notable characteristic of this imposing stranger was his arrogant expression. His head was tilted back like that of a West Point cadet whose cap has slipped down during a parade. He looked down his nose at the assembled players with an imperious sneer, peering scornfully around the room. Obviously, those present were beneath his contempt, for he chose a table and sat down alone. Summoning a waiter with a bad-tempered, ill-bred snap of the fingers, he opened an elaborate red Morocco attaché case and drew out an exquisite backgammon board, on which he began to set up a game, idly rolling the dice by himself.

"Fistula," muttered Sam, in a voice stifled with outrage.

"I beg your pardon?"

"Laszlo Fistula, the shipping magnate."

I looked at the stranger with renewed interest. Everyone has heard of Laszlo Fistula, shipowner, multimillionaire, protector of starlets and ballet dancers, habitué of gambling casinos from Monte Carlo to Macao. And most of all, passionate backgammon enthusiast and inveterate winner.

"So that's Fistula," I said. "I understand he always wins. I guess the old proverb 'Them as has gets' still applies after all. With all his money it would be only fair if he lost once in a while. Isn't he the one who ruined young Crandall and forced him to move to the West Side?"

Sam lowered his eyes. It was obvious that the subject of Crandall was a painful one.

"He's the one, all right," Sam said. "And he does always win. I can forgive him that. It's *how* he wins that is unforgivable."

"You mean he cheats?"

"Yes and no. There's cheating and cheating."

"What does that mean?"

Sam explained to me in detail the Fistula formula for backgammon conquest. He always selected a very young and not too affluent opponent, usually a newcomer and almost always someone who felt marginally insecure amid the grandeur and the wall-to-wall celebrities at Chetwode's. Someone who was overanxious to put his best foot forward, but not quite sure about the best place to put it. As soon as Fistula spotted such a pigeon, he swooped like a peregrine falcon.

"A backgammon bully, in other words," I said.

"Down to the soles of his shoes," Sam replied.

"And once he's selected his victim and cut him out of the herd, what does he do then?" I asked.

"He *impresses* him to death."

"Impresses him?"

"Exactly."

Fistula would summon his victim to his table with a lordly gesture and present his engraved calling card, allowing himself the absolute minimum of a bow, practically a nod, icicles dripping from his eyes. The young man, already half petrified with fear, would sit down across the table, and Fistula would produce his own personal backgammon board, which, he would inform his opponent at once, had been in his family for eleven generations.

"Uses his own board, does he?" I asked.

"Always," Sam said. "And what a board! You should see it."

Fistula's board was inlaid with fourteen-carat gold in a fine filigree pattern, with four massive gold corners. The points were inlaid triangles of lapis lazuli contrasting with gleaming mother-of-pearl. In each corner, just above the gold embossing, was the Fistula monogram and crest, picked out in small diamonds.

"Ostentatious," I suggested.

"Vulgar is a better word," he said, "but that's only the board, which, by the way, has its own fitted leather Cartier case lined in velvet. The dice are even flashier."

"The dice?"

"Each die is a cube-cut pigeon's blood ruby. The spots are seed pearls, sunk to surface level in hollows in the rubies."

"Wow!"

"The men are coins. The blacks are Krugerrands."

"What are Krugerrands?"

"They're South African coins minted from pure gold and weighing exactly an ounce."

"Good Lord! What on earth are the whites?"

"Silver Maria Theresa thalers in perfect mint condition."

"The board must be worth a fortune!"

"It is. Imagine a young fellow faced with a game in which the dice alone would pay his kid's tuition at Brearley for years. The sight and feel of all that opulence turns Fistula's opponents to jelly. They can hardly roll, their hands are shaking so. And as for concentrating on the game, well, the poor devils are hard put to add two and two. Oh that's Fistula's slimy little game all right. He never picks on an adversary his own size and weight."

"But the element of luck. . . ."

"Luck doesn't come into it. Every now and then one of Fistula's victims does hit a lucky streak, but if he shows any chance of winning, Fistula takes action."

"Action? What kind of action?"

"Suddenly one of the Krugerrands mysteriously disappears from the table."

"You mean he steals his own coin?"

"Nobody's ever been able to catch him at it, but that's the way it looks. In the middle of a game that looks like a win for the other guy, Fistula suddenly freezes. His eyes flash fire. He makes an elaborate display of counting the men, and sure enough, a gold coin is missing. He's rich; the other fellow isn't. He owns the game, the other fellow is an outsider. The poor victim breaks out in a cold sweat. Since he's the only suspect, how can he be anything but guilty?"

"And then Fistula accuses him of stealing the coin?"

"Just the opposite. In heavily sarcastic terms he chooses to ignore the incident. He gives his opponent a look that shrivels him to the size of a dried lentil, reaches into his pocket, and replaces the Krugerrand with a penny. But the damage is done. The victim is as limp as a deflated balloon. From then on, he can barely lift the dice cup, much less play an intelligent game. The accusing penny stares up at him. He's afraid to touch the dice for fear one of them will turn up missing, too."

"Poor fellow. I suppose Fistula takes advantage of his condition."

"To the hilt. He takes him for everything he's got. To add insult to injury, the missing coin always turns up at the end, usually on the floor in the vicinity of Fistula's foot."

Fistula's board was inlaid with fourteen-carat gold in a fine filigree pattern with four massive gold corners. The points were inlaid with triangles of lapis lazuli contrasted with gleaming mother-of-pearl. In each corner, just above the gold embossing, was the Fistula monogram and crest, picked out in small diamonds.

"But why does he do it? Surely, playing against that sort of pigeon the stakes can't be very high."

"Not to Fistula, but certainly for the people he plays. He doesn't need the money, but he takes a sadistic pleasure in robbing those who do. He knows that his victims are incapable of facing that board and playing for nickels and dimes. They always bet too much and end up way in over their heads. He loves to watch them squirm and listen to them break."

"The swine! And that's what he did to young Crandall?"

"Yes. Took his apartment, his car, and finally his East Hampton place. His kid had to transfer to P.S. 104."

"No!"

"Yes."

"Something ought to be done about him."

"Yes, but what?"

An idea was forming in my mind. "Suppose," I said, "just suppose that it were possible to give this Fistula a dose of his own medicine."

Sam's eyebrows shot up. "What do you mean?" he asked in a voice trembling with hope.

"Just what I said."

"And how do we go about doing that?"

"Have you ever heard of Channing Bellinghast?"

Sam's face lit up. "Of course," he said. "I certainly have. But can he do it? Fistula won't play with anyone who looks like an equal. And how on earth do we break him down? The man's got an ego of Carborundum steel."

"Leave that to Bellinghast."

A word of explanation, for Bellinghast, though well-known in backgammon circles, may not be so familiar to the world at large. Channing is a man of independent means whose hobby is the discomfiture of backgammon cheats and bullies everywhere. Having once been victimized by a sharper in his youth, he has devoted his life to defending

57

the weak and punishing the wicked of the backgammon world. He asks nothing in return. His is the satisfaction of the big-game hunter who plants a high-velocity magnum .303 slug between the eyes of a man-eating tiger that has been terrorizing a village of frightened natives. He is, so to speak, the Lone Ranger (sans Tonto) of backgammon.

I waved at Luigi, our waiter, and asked him to bring me a blank cablegram form.

Three weeks later, Sam and I walked into the bar at Chetwode's with a slender, dark, youngish man in his forties, elegantly turned out in a Savile Row suit. We sat down at the bar not far from a corner stool upon which Fistula had seated himself so that he could observe the action in the game rooms. He was moodily sipping a Perrier. He sneered when he saw us and paid us no further attention until, at one turn in the conversation, Sam addressed our guest as "Your Highness."

In addition to being a bully, Fistula was a snob. His ears pricked up, and he began to pay close heed to our conversation, which dealt purposefully with international petroleum prices. When Sam turned to him with a cordial smile and asked him to join us, he nearly fell over his feet hurrying to our section of the bar.

"Good evening, Mr. Fistula," Sam said graciously "May I present you to . . . uh . . . well, our guest tonight prefers to remain incognito for reasons of his own. You may simply call him Jim."

"Good evening," said the bogus Jim gravely, graciously inclining himself in Fistula's direction without offering his hand.

Fistula grinned in a conspiratorial but deferential manner. "Good evening, sir," he said, bowing respectfully from the waist.

"I have heard much of you, Mr. Fistula," said our companion. "Your ships, your villa at Cap Ferrat, your many

58

exploits in and out of the business world. You are a figure of some international celebrity."

Fistula blushed modestly and raised a deprecating hand as if to disavow the compliment.

"No, no! My dear sir, you are really quite famous. I am delighted to make your acquaintance."

Fistula beamed with pride.

"And I hear you are something of a gambler, too."

"I occasionally allow myself a small wager, Your High . . . er . . . Jim," Fistula croaked happily. "It passes the time."

"Then perhaps you would join me in a game of backgammon."

It was more than a suggestion and very much akin to a royal command. Fistula's face fell, Jim was obviously no pigeon and certainly not a man to be impressed by the opulence of his equipment. He looked like a tough opponent and one who would not be easily overcome by Fistula's customary steamroller tactics. On the other hand, he was highly flattered by the invitation from such an obviously consequential person. He protested weakly, but Jim merely waved away his objections with a casual but firm gesture.

Sam and I drew up a table and placed four chairs around it. Before he could stop himself, Fistula was sitting across from our guest, who laid a thick packet of new hundred-dollar bills down in front of him.

Fistula reached for his monogrammed case, but Jim shook his head.

"I prefer to use my own board, if you have no objection," he said.

Fistula opened his mouth and then closed it again. Without waiting to see whether Fistula objected or not, our guest produced a battered leather portfolio with a faded coronet on its flap and drew from it a backgammon board, which he laid on the table between them. Fistula glanced at it and his face contorted with rage.

"Is this some sort of joke?" he growled, turning to Sam.

"Not to me," Sam said, "and not to the gentleman who made it."

Fistula looked down at the board again, and this time he started back in amazement. He had placed his hand palm down on the board, but now he drew it back as though he had received an electric shock.

The board consisted of a thin piece of beaverboard with a sheet of heavy paper pasted over it. The points were drawn in uneven lines as though by a child and blocked in in bright colors. It was obviously handmade. The effect was pleasing if unusual.

Fistula was staring at the corner nearest him. On it, in a spidery handwriting, was the signature "Henri Matisse."

"My God!" he whispered.

"Will you roll first?" our guest asked, setting out the men. Fistula gaped at them. The blacks were thin discs of ivory with miniature portraits of Persian cavalrymen on them. The whites were ancient Roman seals bearing the profiles of different emperors in a kind of bisquelike white ceramic.

With a trembling hand, unable to take his eyes off the board, Fistula rolled: a six and two. The dice were small and grayish, made of some semiporous substance with the dots marked in black ink. He looked weakly at Sam, his eyes questioning.

"Relics," Sam whispered. "The knuckle bones of St. Wilhelmina of Lodz. Jim rescued them from behind the Iron Curtain. He feels that they bring him luck."

"The eleventh-century martyr," Fistula muttered, putting the dice cup down with great reverence. He was shaking like a leaf. His face was now alternately parchment white and blotchy purple. He picked up a man to make his move and uttered a cry of horror. The Roman ceramic had disintegrated to powder in his hand.

He began to stammer incoherent apologies, but Jim merely looked at him, reached into his pocket and replaced the piece with a nickel. The wretched Fistula seized his drink and took a deep swallow.

"Please try to control yourself, Mr. Fistula," Jim said. "You are making the devil of a mess out of my board."

Fistula looked down, his jaw dropped, and a pathetic moan of dismay issued from his mouth. A goodly portion of his drink had slopped over onto the board, squiggling down over the delicate colors and blending them into an unattractive blotch about two inches in diameter. Fistula dropped the glass on the floor, where it shattered into splinters.

From then on Fistula played like a man in the last stages of senile dementia. He seemed incapable of decision. He missed the simplest and most obvious advantageous moves. He pushed his men about the board without rhyme or reason, like a malfunctioning automaton.

Our guest, on the other hand, played coolly and brilliantly. By the end of the evening, the sweating Fistula had lost a fortune, including his famous board, which became the property of the false Jim. After the final game, he staggered off into the night without saying goodbye. We never saw him at Chetwode's again.

"It was really quite simple," Channing told us a few nights later as he was handing a check for $50,000 of Fistula's money to young Crandall.

"Not to me," I said. "The white piece that was supposed to be a Roman seal was obviously a forgery made of pressed sugar, which would at some time have crumbled in Fistula's hand. It wasn't really important when it happened. And the miniatures . . ."

"Forgeries, as you suspected. The board was made by

my sister's daughter Amy, age ten. She has a very Matisse-like style. I did the signature myself."

"But how could you have known he would spill his drink? That was a master stroke."

Channing Bellinghast grinned at Sam, who grinned back.

"That was Sam's idea," he said. The simple exchange of a ten-dollar bill with our waiter, Luigi, ensured that Fistula would receive his drink in an ordinary dribble glass, available at any novelty shop in the Times Square area. He couldn't *not* have spilled his drink. Since the board was painted in watercolors, the rest was inevitable. Fistula will never come back to Chetwode's as long as he thinks he might be asked to reimburse me for a Matisse masterpiece."

"I might add," Sam said, "that Luigi returned the ten dollars. He said he would be delighted to do the job for nothing."

"Did he hate Fistula, too?"

"He remembered the game with young Crandall. And one other thing."

"What, for heaven's sake?"

"Luigi came to this country from Europe, where his parents were waiters for generations. He came here so that his children would have opportunities he himself had missed. His son finishes Harvard Law School this year."

"So?"

Sam nodded gravely to Luigi, who was serving a group of players across the room. Luigi, in a most dignified manner, returned Sam's nod.

"If there's one thing Luigi can't stand," Sam said softly, "it's people who snap their fingers at him."

Craft and Arts

The Chic Sheikh appears in many shapes and forms, each more irritating than the last and, alas, Channing Bellinghast is not always there to confound them. If he is male, the fellow may arrive in white breeches and riding boots, carrying a polo mallet. If a woman, she may be clad in a silver lamé jumpsuit with diamanté backgammon points and dice as a motif front and back. The board they use is always too expensive and unique in a way that has little or nothing to do with the game. Instead of a simple contest of luck and skill, backgammon becomes a kind of social one-upmanship.

Don't despair if you can't imitate the style of Matisse. There are other ways to outwit these people. First, spurn their ostentatious equipment. Provide yourself with the cheapest possible Woolworth's cardboard folding backgammon and checkerboard. Plastic men, of course. Kick them around, stamp on them, and work at giving them a suitably battered appearance. Then, when the time is ripe, produce your shabby equipment and tell your snobbish opponent that the set was given to you on your twenty-first birthday by your dying grandmother, and that it is your "lucky" set. You never play with any other. Or get a board made of tin, bang a few dents in it, and tell your adversary that you had it in your shirt front on the Ploesti raid and it saved your life by deflecting a murderous piece of shrapnel.

Bob Wilberforce, with whom I used to play an occasional cheerful game down in Palm Beach, an area literally crawling with Chic Sheikh types, had an excellent way of cutting them down to size. He took an ordinary fountain pen, removed its insides, and inserted a small tape recorder that made a rhythmic beeping sound. If his opponent looked as though he or she might turn out to be a pest of the sort we have been discussing, Bob would set off the beeper. He would then stop the game, pull out the pen, excuse himself, and start talking into it.

"Hello! Hello! Tango-six here," he would say. "How do you read? Right, chief. Coming in loud and clear." This last would always accompany a gesture in which he held the pen close to his ear. A conversation would then ensue in which certain clues would make it obvious to the listener that the person at the other end was you-know-who in the White House. Bob would advise him on the fluidity of the international currency market, the advisability of the sale of B-52's to Iran, the Panama Canal issue, or some such knotty question. Then, with a hearty "So long, Mr. President!" he would return the pen to his pocket, turn to his astounded opponent, and say, "All right! Now where were we?"

It never failed.

6

The Hand That Rocks the Cradle Can Also Deal Out a Cauliflower Ear

Women, as Somerset Maugham's Charles Strickland said a few generations ago, are strange little beasts. You can (according to Strickland) beat them until your arm aches, and they still love you.

Nowadays, there would probably be a good deal of strenuous objection in certain circles to Strickland's pronouncement, or to be more precise, that of the late Mr. Maugham, who was always highly suspicious of females. In the last decade, women have achieved a great deal of well-deserved equality in many fields of endeavor formerly dominated by men. By and large, this equality has been a good thing, but in some cases the ability to occupy positions once considered to be exclusively male has resulted in women absorbing some of the nastier masculine prerogatives as well. I refer specifically to what would formerly have been called the "unladylike" behavior involved in playing cutthroat, rotten, brass-knuckled, underhanded backgammon.

Backgammon is a game (unlike tossing the caber or weightlifting) at which both sexes can play with equal expertise and with an equal chance of winning. A man can play a game or two with the girl of his dreams, secure in the knowledge that he doesn't have to let her win in order to retain her interest and esteem, a humiliating position for both parties.

In spite of the liberation of recent years, there are still attributes peculiar to the female of the species which can sometimes be used to help along the odds. Mind you, I am not accusing women of using femininity to cheat. I would never do that. But sometimes . . . well, consider the Safety Pin Stratagem.

In this chapter we shall see how liberated, modern young women use their new freedom plus the outmoded attitudes of a number of male chauvinists to gain certain ends. If you are a New Woman and the man you're playing with thinks you're an Old-Fashioned Girl, you have all the advantages. Add a little clever cheating, and you can't lose. Men have been underestimating women for centuries. Nowadays, males have learned that regarding females as inferiors, even at backgammon, is a bad mistake.

The Jill-the-Ripper Diversion

The first time I ever heard of the Jill-the-Ripper Diversion, I was consuming a stinger at the swimming pool bar of the Montezuma Bath and Tennis Club in Houston. Around me, in strident tones, tall Texans debated the state of the cattle and cotton markets. White-haired tycoons, burned mahogany by the sun, discussed oil leases. It was a new world for me and I found it fascinating. The fact that I was a stranger seemed to stimulate in my Texan acquaintances a veritable mania for competitive hospitality.

Before I had finished my stinger, I had received a number of invitations, including one for dinner that evening. I accepted with pleasure.

Later on, when dinner was over and my host and I sat in his River Oaks drawing room sipping his excellent brandy the talk turned to backgammon. We spoke of cheats and rascals, notable historic games, outstanding wagers, and other matters. At last, my host refilled my snifter, sat back, and told me the story of young Jillian Mallory and her famous contest, now securely imbedded in Texas legend along with Spindletop, the Battleship Texas, and the Alamo.

The Jill-the-Ripper Diversion was put over by Jillian Mallory on a crafty oil tycoon who pays a man fifty thousand dollars a year to keep his name out of books like this one; and who am I to violate his rule and possibly cost that poor flack his well-paid job?

Jill was an advertising copywriter and part-time photographer's model, pretty as a picture and all sweet curved lines and creamy velvet skin and dark-red hair and green eyes and occasional little dustings of freckles in just the right places. In short, a beauty. And smart, too. It made a man feel, when he looked at her, as though the world wasn't such a bad place after all. That was under normal everyday conditions. But seeing her at the Montezuma in a very small bikini bathing suit, well, that was the sort of thing that caused Paris to hand the golden apple to the wrong lady, got Tristan stabbed in the back, put Lancelot out of the running for the Holy Grail, kept Abelard from settling down with some nice girl and raising a family, and a lot more.

The oilman fixed his rheumy middle-aged eyes on Jill and that was that. He wanted her, and he was a man who always got what he wanted, *pronto!* He went after her with every weapon at his command, but Jill wasn't having any. You see, he was a married man, and she had rules about that. At last, having tried everything else and having been rejected each time, the oilman played his trump card. He appealed to her sporting instinct. This was a wise move, for nowhere in the world is the sporting instinct so highly developed as in the hearts of Texan women.

The ground rules were these: They would meet at poolside at the club and play best two games out of three, no doubling, no extra score for gammons or backgammons, only win or lose. If Jill won, she would receive full title to a parcel of west Texas real estate containing twenty working oil wells. If she lost—well, if that happened, she had to spend a week in Acapulco with the winner.

How could she refuse a sporting proposition like that?

On the appointed afternoon Jill appeared looking even lovelier than usual in her tiny bikini. Her skin was burnished golden tan, and there was scarlet polish on her small, regular toenails. Her eyes were very wide. It was a tense moment. After all, the tycoon had plenty of oil wells, but Jill only had one virtue.

Her opponent spread a large towel at the tiled edge of the pool and placed the board in the center of it. He and Jill knelt facing each other and cast for first roll. Ordinarily, such a contest would have drawn a large audience, but at Jill's request (sacred, with a lady's honor at stake) the usual swimmers and players left them alone on their side of the water.

The first game was touch and go. Both players put every ounce of energy into the play. With a superhuman effort of will and concentration, Jill managed to best the oilman, blocking him with a clever prime at first and then getting her men off with lightning speed and an incredible string of doubles.

She was one ahead. Only one more and she was home free.

In the second game, Jill was forced to wonder whether all that propaganda they hand you in church about good triumphing over evil had any substance to it. The oilman's luck was almost supernatural; every roll of his dice was perfect, while she couldn't seem to do anything right. She lost badly.

The third game began quite normally with the players favored equally by the fickle ivories. But when the end was in sight, a series of fabulously lucky rolls left the oilman with his final two men on his one point. Jill still had four men left. The board looked like this:

JILL

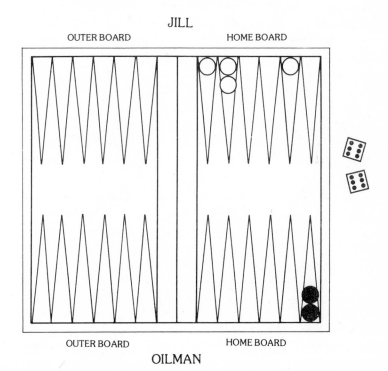

OILMAN

It looked like curtains for our heroine. Any roll of the dice would allow him to take his men off and give him the winning second game, whereas the odds against her rolling double sixes, the only combination that would win for her, were thirty-five to one. It was her roll. If she failed to roll two sixes, it meant . . .

She lowered her eyes and reached for the dice cup.

A large bead of perspiration rolled down the oilman's nose. There was a sore place on his lower lip where he'd bitten through the skin. Jill appeared to be quite calm.

As she leaned forward to grasp the dice cup the silence was broken by the unmistakable sibilant sound of tearing cloth. With a squeal of dismay, Jill dropped the dice and clutched at her bikini, wildly trying to cover both her top and bottom, fore and aft, with her two hands, not an easy job for a full-grown woman as any girl who has been in the same situation can testify. The oilman's eyes popped and his cigar dropped from his gaping mouth.

"Look away! Look the other way, quick! You . . . you *peeping Tom!*" Jill shrieked, scrunching herself into a tiny ball.

There is no insult more painful to a Texan than one that suggests that with respect to the pleasures of the flesh his enjoyments might be, shall we say, a bit kinky. Wounded to the quick by the words "peeping Tom" and trained from boyhood in the basic conduct required of gentlemen, the oilman rapidly averted his eyes. A few seconds later Jill said, "All right. I'm decent. You can look now."

Sure enough, the bikini was quite intact, as it had been earlier. She had adjusted or repaired whatever the damage had been.

"Let's get on with the game," said her greedy would-be lover. "It's your roll. Hurry up and lose so we can get on down to Mexico!"

The silence was broken by the unmistakable sound of tearing cloth. Jill dropped the dice and clutched at her bikini. "Look away . . . look the other way quick, you . . . you peeping Tom!"

"I'm afraid the game is over," Jill said, pointing to the board where her dice cup had fallen. The satanic little cubes lay on the board face up showing a double six, the only possible roll that could have won her the game!

Practitioners of the Jill-the-Ripper Diversion know, of course, that before kneeling on the towel at the beginning of the game, our heroine had placed a small square of cotton cloth about the size of a handkerchief under her knee. When the time came, as it inevitably must come in backgammon, when it is essential to divert your opponent's attention from the dice, she knelt down hard on the cloth as she leaned her weight forward, extending her right hand for the dice cup, and ripped the cloth upward with her left hand. Her subsequent pantomime naturally led the oilman to believe that it was her scanty costume that had given way. As any good sleight-of-hand man will tell you, the hand is quicker than the eye, and people will believe what they *want* to believe.

The oilman was no fool. He smelled a rat, but there wasn't a thing he could do about it. Jill sold her oil property six months later and bought a pretty, ranch-style house in River Oaks. She married young Bill Waterman who worked at the office with her. The two of them quit Smith, Smith, Baldwin & Carlsberg and opened their own advertising agency with the remainder of her oil money. When last heard of, they were doing very well.

The Heavy Husband Hoax

The Heavy Husband Hoax is as successful as the Jill-the-Ripper Diversion. This bit of skulduggery requires an exceptionally large and dangerous-looking husband or boy friend to back up a lady player's use of female firepower in confusing a male opponent.

Just such a bruiser is "Big Eddie" Kronowski, former right guard of the Rhode Island Lemmings and now a man to reckon with in the municipal bond market. Eddie stands six feet seven in his size eighteen socks. Four years of vigorous line play distributed his nose over most of the middle part of his face. His hands look like those medium-sized legs of lamb stamped 'New Zealand' that you see in supermarket freezers. In short, Eddie is not a man you would care to antagonize—or even to look askance at—when he is in a bad mood.

He is married to svelte Nedda Kronowski, who loves backgammon passionately.

It was during a game with Charlie Porter, top-ranking dice roller of the Nutmeg Racquet Club in Hartford that Nedda first conceived and brought to a successful conclusion the now-famous Heavy Husband Hoax.

She and Charlie were sitting on a sofa in the club lounge, facing one another with the board between them. Nedda had slipped off her shoes and tucked her feet under her. Her knees were about two inches apart, and her skirt was smoothed over her thighs in a thoroughly ladylike manner. Nedda's husband, Eddie, was across the room, comfortably ensconced in a leather armchair absorbing the wisdom of *Sports Illustrated.*

Charlie and Nedda were playing California rules, which means that dice rolling off the board (which was a small one) would be played according to the number shown face up regardless of where they happened to lie, unless, of course, one or both of them were cocked or leaning against some object. In that case, they would be, naturally, rolled again.

On several occasions during the game the dice had rolled onto the floor. The two players would wait until they came to rest and would play them as they lay, after which Charlie, always the gentleman, would get up from the sofa and retrieve them.

At one particularly crucial moment in the game, Nedda faced disaster doubled unless she could produce a high double. She took the dice cup and shook it. The municipal-bond market was down and there was a considerable wager involved. Raising her eyes heavenward, she rolled, but not quite hard enough. Instead of rolling on the board, the cubes struck the edge of it and rebounded in Nedda's direction, traveling directly into the two-inch space between her knees, under her skirt, and coming to rest at a point where, a decade ago, they would have been parallel to her garters.

Charlie looked at Nedda. Then he looked at her knees and the place just above them where the now-invisible dice were hiding. Then he hazarded a glance at Big Eddie who was still engrossed in his magazine.

"Roll again," he said.

"Not on your life," Nedda said. "You know the rules. They're good unless they're cocked and these aren't touching anything. I'll play them as they are."

"Well, stand up very slowly and let's see them."

"I *can't* do that! If I move at all they'll tumble around. Do you want to reach in and get them?"

Charlie looked over at Eddie again and swallowed nervously.

"No," he said, "but I can't see them."

"I'm not yanking my skirt up to my hips for your amusement. Eddie doesn't like that sort of thing. Hold on a minute, though. I've got an idea."

She took a small mirror from her purse and held it in front of her knees, facing toward her.

"Game!" she said cheerfully, scooping out the dice and throwing them into the cup. Charlie opened his mouth, but just then Eddie appeared, putting his arm around his wife's pretty shoulders.

"How're you doing, Hon?"

"We just finished and *look!*" she said, giving him a

delighted squeeze and giving him the fistful of currency she had just taken from Charlie.

Charlie says he was reminded of the scene in *Guys and Dolls* in which Big Julie of violent reputation wins the crap game by rolling the dice in his derby. In life, as in backgammon, Charlie says, there is a time for prudence and a time for calculated risk. He now plays only with single women or those with very small husbands.

Getting Even

You must not get the impression from these examples that women *always* win, even when they lower themselves to the point of using less than honorable tactics. There are men in this world, thank heaven, who not only understand women but who can still outthink them and outplay them.

One of these is Arthur Belknap. Years of bachelorhood and games of chance with women on three continents developed in him a fine appreciation of the qualities of the female brain. A man of charm, intelligence, good looks, and independent income, Arthur has been for some years a target of opportunity for unmarried women. He has seen all the tricks, and he knows every thrust, parry, and riposte. He is also a top-notch backgammon player. Some of his spur-of-the-moment defenses against female trickery are now backgammon history.

For example, in a crucial game with lovely Dinah Merlin, formerly the prettiest drum majorette at school and much improved a decade later, Arthur was facing a critical play when he heard his bewitching partner murmur, "Oops! There goes my darned safety pin!" He rose at once, strode to a nearby piano, whipped a large cashmere shawl from its top, and draped it around the astounded Dinah like a cape, enveloping her from head to toe. Then he bowed gracefully and continued the game to its victorious (for him) close.

Approaching a critical point in a game with Eleanor Freundlich, whose husband, "Iron Jim" Freundlich, had taught hand-to-hand combat to the Fourth Marine Division, Arthur showed no surprise when Ellie's faulty throw caused the dice to carom off the board and under her skirt between her rosy knees. Reaching into his breast pocket, he produced in rapid succession (1) a pair of surgical forceps with which he lifted the hem of her skirt three-quarters of an inch; (2) a dentist's mirror with a long folding handle which he inserted under her skirt so that the angled mirror faced forward, reflecting only the cubes and the surface of the cushion; and (3) a Monte Carlo style croupier's rake, with which he scooped the dice back into play after reading out the unassuming two and one that they showed.

"With a two and one," he said, "I'm afraid I'm going to have to double you."

In a beachside game with captivating Helen Forester, a sultry Southern beauty famous for wearing the smallest bathing costumes at the Maidstone Club, he turned the doubling cube at a critical moment. As Helen leaned forward to pick up the dice, she fumbled under her left knee briefly. The sound of ripping cloth was heard.

"Look the other way, *quick!*" Helen shrieked. But Arthur only smiled.

"No need," he said. "Your modesty is perfectly safe with me. Lost my contact lenses this morning. Blind as a bat without them. Can't see more than a foot at the most. It's all I can do to read the dice or tell the reds from the whites."

A champion of champions was Arthur. Up to a point.

What finally finished off old Arthur was his contest with Marion Waldrop in the club's mixed semifinals. Marion appeared for the game dressed in a white blouse and neat black cashmere sweater, with snug beige slacks and small patent-leather low-heeled shoes. Her ash-blond hair was brushed back and held with a rose-colored ribbon. She wore almost no makeup. She was exceptionally pretty, but there was a no-nonsense air of brisk efficiency about her. It put Arthur on his guard at once.

He mentally rehearsed all his antifemale chicanery equipment, but uselessly. He never needed it. Although Marion was a brilliant player—one of the best in the club—he beat her rapidly, three out of three.

At every critical roll he tensed, ready for trickery, but it never came.

At the end of the third game she looked up at him. A large silvery tear rolled down her silken cheek.

"I think you're the most wonderful backgammon player I've ever *seen,*" she said. "You made me look like a silly fool. I'll never play again as long as I live."

Never play backgammon again?

"There, there," said Arthur, for want of something better to say. A crushing load of guilt descended on his shoulders. He pulled out his handkerchief and dabbed at the tear, which promptly released a cascade of fresh ones. Somehow, Arthur was never able to figure out just how her blond head found its way to his chest, where it sobbed against the cloth of his jacket.

"You're so *kind,* so *gentle,*" Marion murmured into his collarbone.

Two months later they were married. Marion did play backgammon again, of course. She plays it frequently with Arthur, beating him two out of three times, fair and square and no tricks. She's one of those natural players with a mind like a 360-series IBM computer.

After his twentieth defeat, Arthur began to wonder whether or not he'd been the victim of a feminine stratagem for which he hadn't been prepared. He was reminded of the Lincoln-Douglas debate in which Honest Abe deliberately threw a congressional election in order to insure victory in the presidential contest to come.

"After all," Arthur says to anyone who will listen to him, "it doesn't matter whether you win or lose, as long as you play the game."

"Yes, dear," Marion says, squeezing his hand.

Backgammon for Lovers

It isn't always women, liberated or not, who use the difference between the sexes to confuse backgammon adversaries. Men can play at that game, too. Take the example of Albert McWhinney, who found himself listed on the East Sewickley Country Club bulletin board as semifinalist in the annual backgammon mixed singles last September. When he realized who his opposite number would be, his heart skipped a beat. The name on the chart next to his was Binkie Goldsmith!

Admittedly, Binkie has outstanding mental and physical qualities. No one has ever tried to deny that. But in Albert's eyes, she was undoubtedly the most beautiful, wonderful, desirable woman in the world. Albert was, for the first time in his young life, head over heels in love.

This presented a dilemma. Can a man in love force the object of his affections to accept a humiliating defeat in a backgammon tournament and run the risk of losing her forever? On the other hand, can such a man degrade his sweetheart by playing down to her, letting her win, throwing the game, so to speak, and thus earning her contempt? Either way he would lose her (although, Albert realized, the first decision would somewhat alleviate the loss by giving him a crack at the finals). What to do? It never occurred to

Albert that Binkie might beat him for the simple reason that she might prove to be the better player.

On the day of the semifinals, Albert had made his decision. He sat down opposite Binkie in the game room of the club and using his thumbnail, calmly cracked the plastic wrapping on a brand-new backgammon set. Binkie was wearing a new dress that matched her eyes, and she was looking especially fetching. Albert regarded her with approval. He opened the board between them and handed her a dice cup.

As time passed, Albert won two games and Binkie won two. Then they began the final and crucial game. Binkie had the black men, and as Albert was setting up the board, he removed one and substituted another black piece, undistinguishable from the original. On her third roll, Binkie picked up the new man to move it. To her surprise, it flew open in her hand. Inside it, in a nest of pink velvet, was a three-carat diamond engagement ring. Her eyes popped.

"Wow!" she said. Albert looked shyly down at the table.

"I love you," he whispered.

It isn't every day a girl gets a proposal of marriage. Regardless of the advancement of one's state of liberation or the height of one's consciousness, it can be an earth-shaking experience. Binkie was thoroughly rattled.

"I . . . uh . . . don't know what to say," she said. She looked around to see if anyone had noticed. "This is so . . . so *unexpected!*"

Albert took her hand and kissed it. Then he picked up her dice.

"No one else shall ever play with dice that have been used by that adorable hand," he said, and with that he slipped them into his mouth and swallowed them.

Binkie reached out to stop him, but it was too late.

From that moment, Binkie's full attention was on the prospect of marriage to Albert, her silver pattern, where they would live, whether three cars were really necessary—everywhere but on the game. Albert shared his dice with her but she seemed to be playing in a daze. He won and went on to take the finals and trophy.

Of course, the dice were fakes, made of candy. Albert had substituted them for the real ones before the last game. Whether Binkie realized this at the time is hard to say. In any event, if she did, she has never admitted it. And she never complained about losing the semifinals, either.

"What difference does it make?" she says. "It's only a game." She's a philosophical sort of girl.

Backgammon only a game? That remark seems more suited to an Old-Fashioned Girl than to a New Woman, but does anything really matter as long as love conquers all?

7
That Old Black Magic

By this time, the reader, if he or she has been paying attention, has absorbed a good deal of information about backgammon scoundrels and their methods and motivations. The reader has learned as well how to prepare for, identify, and combat a number of backgammon skulduggeries, just as a black belt judo-ka uses his adversary's own weight to topple him onto the mat.

I hope so.

But let me warn you. The examples so far are only the beginning. There is worse to come. The ways of the backhanded backgammon practitioner (as Channing Bellinghast often says) are as the stars in the Milky Way, myriad and as yet uncounted.

Now You See It

Take for example an experience I had in Hong Kong some years ago, more years ago than I care to enumerate. Remember, this could happen to you!

Hong Kong is, as everyone knows, the brightest jewel (in fact the *only* jewel) in the British Imperial diadem. The last of the great colonies, it retains much of the charming and almost Victorian formality of the halcyon days of the Raj and the Concessions. People still dress for dinner after six. Slippered Shanghai servants pad about dressed in blue pajamas or white mess jackets, pampering their masters. Rickshaw boys run through the narrow streets towing a very occasional official in a solar topee (the British much prefer to travel by air-conditioned taxi, except when photographers are about) and a great number of American sailors, passengers of cruise ships, and expensive ladies of the evening. Snatches of mysterious polyphonic Chinese music escape from shuttered windows in the Wanchai district. Hong Kong and the distant Communist mountains, checkered with glittering rice paddies, are so exquisite that you can spend a week there before you stop noticing them.

I was charged with some government mission or other, now stuffed away in a forgotten file, but dreadfully important at the time. After I had signed the book at Government House and looked in at the office of the dignitary whose instructions I carried in my briefcase, I made the routine call on the consul-general, who invited me to lunch.

While we shared an excellent *kung pao chi ting*, washed down with the best grade of Chinese rice wine (the kind that tastes like California sherry) on the consul's Peak-perched terrace, we chatted idly about American politics, the latest books, the London and New York theater seasons, and the latest scandals, which were pretty much the same as the ancient ones.

"By the way," he said, "I got these for you as soon as I heard you were coming." He handed me a sheaf of guest cards that conveyed temporary membership for me in the Hong Kong Club, the Royal Hong Kong Yacht Club, the Correspondents' Club, and a few others. I thanked him.

"I understand you're a backgammon player," he said. "I'd be careful about the people I played with here, if I were you. We get some strange types washed ashore here in the Colony. Adventurers of all sorts. Never know what you might be getting into, if you know what I mean. One hears stories."

I assured him that at least in this respect I was perfectly capable of looking after myself.

"I hope so," he said, unconvinced.

In a day or two, when I had completed my business, I dropped in at the Correspondents' Club at lunchtime. I ordered a gimlet and carried it out to the terrace in order to enjoy the sunshine and the fine view of the harbor and Kowloon. A number of members had preceded me, some of whom I recognized as representatives of the major news agencies. I knew one or two of them and soon we were buying rounds of drinks and planning the evening's entertainment. The waiter kept us well supplied, and a group of us sat down to lunch together.

As the lunch hour drew to a close, I saw a tall, dark saturnine man step out onto the terrace from the club reading room. His sober black suit contrasted the rumpled white ducks of my press friends. He wore a white silk turban and affected a neatly trimmed moustache and beard, black tinged with gray.

Wilson of the *Times*, who was unsuccessfully trying to pump me about the details of my mission, followed my gaze and identified the newcomer.

"Padwar Singh," he said. "*Times of India*. Odd sort. Very odd."

"An understatement if I ever heard one," said Ransome of the *Express*. The man's not odd; he's positively uncanny."

"Not so uncanny as all that," said an attaché of the Swedish Consulate. "He's a Chinese agent."

Wilson shrugged. "In any event, he gives me the creeps, I don't mind telling you."

"He's doesn't look all that odd to me," I admitted.

"You don't know him," Wilson explained. "They say," lowering his voice, "he has *powers.*"

"Powers?" I must confess that my curiosity was piqued.

"You know," Wilson laughed an embarrassed little laugh, "magic. The rope trick. That sort of thing."

"Magic? You mean he does party tricks?"

"He does tricks all right," the Swedish attaché said ruefully. "He took me for a hundred and fifty dollars at backgammon last week. My wife was furious. American dollars, of course. It was almost supernatural the way the dice work for him."

"Do you mean he uses crooked dice?" I asked.

"How can you use crooked dice in backgammon? A player can't tell in advance what combinations are needed. Besides, if he weighted them to come up double five or six more frequently than other combinations, it would be obvious to his opponent, not to mention deleterious to his own game. No, it wasn't loaded dice. It was something quite different. When I played with him, the dice kept coming up at exactly the numbers he needed to hit my men or move his into his home board or to construct an inescapable trap for me."

"Maybe he's just lucky," I suggested. "It's been known to happen and not only at backgammon."

"Nobody has *that* kind of luck," Wilson said sourly, speaking from the experience of a life-long newsman who knew what he was talking about.

As the lunch hour wore on into late afternoon, the press people drifted off to their offices. At length, I found myself sitting alone on the terrace except for the dark presence of Padwar Singh who was reading in the background, alone at his table. Almost as though he had been waiting for the last newsman to leave, he laid down his *China News,* rose to his feet, and came to my corner of the terrace. By way of introduction, he explained that he had read some of my backgammon books and articles.

"Are you an enthusiast, then?" I asked him.

"Indeed I am, sir. I play as often as I can find a suitable opponent, a high-quality player," he said.

Not all that often, I thought, remembering the Swedish attaché. Nevertheless, I was intrigued by the man's reputation. I felt an overwhelming desire to see those magic dice in action.

As though he had read my mind, Padwar Singh suggested that we try a game. He sat down opposite me on the terrace, facing the magnificent gardens of the villas on the Peak, and sent the waiter to fetch a board.

I found Padwar Singh to be an experienced and conservative player. He knew exactly what he was about and had a set pattern of strategy, which he followed without rashness or undue risk. There appeared to be nothing unusual about the behavior of the dice nor about the way he moved his men. Alert for any sign of cheating, I saw none. He was a pleasant and engaging companion. In spite of my friends' warnings, I found myself liking him, enjoying his company very much.

After several games, we each had won and lost an approximately equal number of Hong Kong dollars, which were the stakes. We seemed to be evenly matched. Padwar Singh suggested a higher wager to make the game more interesting. "Here it comes," I said to myself, resolved to be doubly watchful. I agreed to play for U.S. dollars.

As afternoon became evening, the wagers grew larger. By sundown, I found myself accepting a double that brought the stakes up to five dollars a point while the doubling cube was standing at sixteen. A lot of money if I lost.

Padwar Singh shook the dice cup thoughtfully. He rolled a double five, sending two of my poor chaps to the bar and moving the last of his men into striking distance of his home board.

I stared. There was nothing out of the ordinary in his move, and yet I could have sworn I had had no men skulking about in exposed positions, especially as I was ahead in what was essentially a running game. It would have been the most arrant idiocy! How could I forget two stark naked men?

It wasn't long before I rolled a combination that allowed me to bring my men off the bar. I reached for a piece but started back in amazement. What I had thought was an empty point was neatly blocked by two of Padwar Singh's men!

Of course, it was not impossible for me to be in error. Everyone makes mistakes. Under the pressure of so high a bet it was understandable that I might overlook a blot or a blocked point. But *two* major mistakes in a row? I was far too experienced at the game for anything like that to happen. Could the man really have magical powers? Could it be a kind of hypnosis as the rope trick is explained to be?

I scrutinized him closely. I had not taken my eyes off him since the first wager, except to follow the dice. While I was watching the dice, could he have moved his men? One of his hands was occupied with a long Filipino cheroot and the other held a tall glass of some brownish carbonated beverage. He would have had to get rid of one or the other in order to cheat in that way, and I was certain he hadn't.

Whether he had magical powers or not, it was only minutes before Padwar Singh bore his last man home and won a large wad of my banknotes. I never play for more than I can afford to lose, but I had planned to visit Tokyo and Taipei on my way home. Padwar Singh's victory put a definite crimp in the pleasures I expected to enjoy in those capitals. With a sigh I bade him farewell and returned to my room at the Peninsula.

"I told you so," the consul general said next morning. " 'Be careful who you gamble with in Hong Kong,' I said, but no. You could take care of yourself, you said. Well, don't say I didn't warn you." He seemed elated to have been proven correct and by my punishment for ignoring his warning.

To take the odor of defeat out of my nostrils, I walked down Garden Road from the consulate-general and took the ferry back to Kowloon, where I proposed to buy a cashmere jacket at Mohan's. The cheerful fitters danced around me with their tape measures, making chalk marks and thrusting drinks into my hand as they complimented me on my good taste in choosing such an establishment and such a remarkable bolt of cloth. There is nothing like a Hong Kong tailor's shop for lifting the flagging spirits.

As I was being bowed out the door by Mohan's enormous staff of employees and relatives, I nearly collided with a slim, youngish, dark-haired man in his forties, dressed in crisp white linen and a Coffee House tie.

"Channing Bellinghast!" I cried, wringing his hand.

Bellinghast (for it was indeed the backgammon Galahad himself) expressed his delight at finding an old friend so far from home in the last outpost of Empire. He explained that he was pausing to replenish his wardrobe en route home from a journey to Calcutta. In no time at all we were sharing a table and a friendly whisky and soda in the Palm Court of the Peninsula Hotel. I told him about my misadventure with Padwar Singh. Bellinghast looked very grave.

"I have a strong desire to meet this magical gentleman," he said, frowning. "There is something about him that arouses my curiosity."

"And mine, to my cost," I said. "But nothing is simpler.

Come to the Correspondents' Club with me at four this afternoon when most of the members will have left for work. He's usually alone there at that time. God knows when he goes to his office, assuming he has one."

The meeting occurred almost as though I had planned it in advance. Padwar Singh was sitting alone as usual, and since the other members had left, he shared the terrace with Liu, the waiter, who was mopping the recently-vacated tables with a plastic sponge. Down in the harbor, an American president liner was flying the blue peter next to a rusting coaster, whose unintelligible name was painted on her hull in Cyrillic letters. Padwar Singh smiled as though he had been expecting us and rose to his feet.

"Have you come to take your revenge?" he asked me.

"No, only to introduce my friend Mr. McIntire to the facilities of the club."

McIntire was the name Bellinghast had chosen for his meeting with Padwar Singh. He purported to be a manufacturer of women's garments, in Hong Kong on a textile-buying mission.

Padwar Singh examined him closely. Then, apparently satisfied with what he saw, he suggested a drink, sticking to his usual nonalcoholic cola beverage. Half an hour later he had invited "McIntire" to play a friendly game of backgammon—with a small wager "to make the game more interesting."

My friend accepted, naturally. He sat down opposite Padwar Singh, and Liu brought the game from its cupboard. "McIntire" drew a cigarette case and lighter from his pocket and laid them before him near a stack of currency. A fresh round of drinks appeared; the game was on.

Since I was the only person not occupied, I wandered to the edge of the terrace and watched the big ships loading and unloading in the harbor, the hundreds of junks and sampans plying the narrow area between Hong Kong and

Kowloon. Soon Wilson and Ransome entered, accompanied by Fredericks of the *Chronicle.*

"Our weird friend has found another pigeon, it seems," Wilson observed.

"He's no pigeon," I said. "He's a friend of mine, Bob McIntire of Cleveland. Dress manufacturer."

"You never learn, do you?" Ransome said bitterly. "We tried to warn you off him but you had to try for yourself. You lost your money, and now you've let your friend in for an expensive whitewashing as well."

"I don't think so," I said. "McIntire can look after himself."

"So could you, or so you said."

"Look at that!" Wilson said suddenly. "It looks as though he's taken your pal to the cleaners, too."

Sure enough, Padwar Singh was smiling and apologizing profusely for winning as he accepted a fat wad of banknotes, which Channing Bellinghast had just removed from an alligator billfold. The backgammon Galahad was politely waving away the apologies. The two men rose from their table. With a bow, Padwar Singh turned and headed for the French doors that led from the terrace into the interior of the club.

"Good God!" Wilson croaked, his eyes bulging. "Will you look at that!"

Channing Bellinghast's cigarette case and lighter had leaped off the table. They were following Padwar Singh toward the exit. The Sikh turned slowly and looked at them. His mouth dropped open. He tried to get away, but the two objects reached him first and rose gracefully from the floor, describing an arc through the air, and fastened themselves to his right leg. He screamed and flailed at them, babbling something in a language I didn't understand.

"Now I've seen everything," Ransome whispered in awe.

Bellinghast's cigarette case and lighter had leaped off the table and were following Padwar Singh toward the exit. He screamed and flailed at them, babbling something in a language I didn't understand.

A Spanish vice-consul who had just come in crossed himself devoutly.

Channing Bellinghast seemed to be the only person who was not surprised. He walked up to Padwar Singh and retrieved his property from the fellow's trouser leg. Then he held out his hand firmly. The Sikh reached into his pocket and produced Channing's losses and an equal sum of his own and placed the money in my friend's palm. Then he turned away, shoulders sagging, and left the room.

"It was just as I suspected," Bellinghast explained to us later in the bar. "He made Liu bring him the same board every time. Since he was lavish with his tips, Liu had no reason to suspect anything improper was going on."

"There'll be some changes made around here," Wilson said, with a malevolent glance in Liu's direction.

"It wasn't Liu's fault," my friend said. "He thought Padwar Singh had magical powers, too."

"And how did he do it?" Ransome asked.

"Each of the men, instead of being simply made of red or black plastic, had a thin disc of steel inserted into it. Singh had a small, high-powered magnet strapped to his right knee under his trousers. When his adversary's attention was distracted, he could, by bringing his knee up close to the table underneath a given man, move that man from one point to another without using his hands."

"The scoundrel!"

"In that way, he could leave blots or block his own or his opponents' points, or even return men that had been sent to the bar."

"It sounds so simple, now that you've explained it," Wilson said. "Mind if I send in a story to the *Times*?"

The backgammon Galahad looked at him, alarmed. "Please don't," he said, "it would make my mission much more difficult than it already is. In many cases, my success in destroying backgammon cheats is due to my anonymity."

Wilson nodded. "Your secret is safe with us," he said, glancing around at the other correspondents, who voiced entire agreement.

"But how did you do that last bit of business with the cigarette case and lighter," I asked.

"When you told me your story this morning, I suspected at once what Singh was up to. I took the precaution of substituting a stainless-steel case and lighter for my usual silver ones. I then carried them over to the physics laboratory at Hong Kong University and asked an old friend of mine who teaches there to fit them with a small electromagnet, which I could turn on or off when necessary.

He drew the two objects in question from his pocket and handed them to Wilson. "For Liu, the waiter," he said, "to compensate a little for his loss of face in helping a scoundrel unwittingly. In any event, I would never be able to take them home with me. They would throw off the compass and other instruments of any airliner."

"Incredible!" I said.

Padwar Singh was posted on the club bulletin board the same day, but he never returned. He was seen once or twice in some of the less savory haunts of Wanchai, and then a few weeks later he disappeared entirely. Unmasked as a cheat, he could no longer use his club memberships to drive his adversaries into debt and blackmail them into releasing information of value to his Chinese Communist superiors or his editors in Delhi, who had no idea he was an intelligence agent.

Some say he returned home to India and was given some innocuous job on the paper there. One rumor held that the infamous Second Bureau of the People's Republic of China felt that he had outlived his usefulness and merely eliminated him. No one ever found out which was the true story.

"Poor devil!" I said.

"That is the Orient for you," Bellinghast said. "And besides, when one stoops to cheating at backgammon, one gets what one deserves."

Undoubtedly, Bellinghast is right, when you come right down to it.

Of course, Channing Bellinghast is a special sort of man with special skills. He is more than equipped to cope with highbinders, even if they have a direct line to the occult. But what if Channing isn't there to help you? What if you are on your own and you come up against an opponent who has *powers?*

Crystal Ball Chicanery

Let's look at what happened to Dan O'Shaughnessy, bartender at Hoge's in Indianapolis. Dan had been a bartender since the 1930s, and you would think that in forty-odd years on the job he would have run into every known type of eccentric, and you'd probably be right. But Dan had a weakness. Being a fine old Irishman, he believed in witches, fairies, banshees, vampires, and every other sort of storybook weirdie. The little people were very real to him and his world was full of them. They were easy to blame for whatever good or bad luck befell him on or off the job.

One day, as he was polishing glasses during an early afternoon lull, he overheard a customer talking about the Mental Marvel. Immediately his ears pricked up.

"Don't know how he does it," the customer was saying. "He just seems to read people's minds. Knows what you're thinking before you start thinking it."

"Who? What?" Dan wanted to know.

"This Mental Marvel. He plays backgammon. Keeps a crystal ball next to the board. He looks into the crystal before the other guy rolls and knows what he's going to roll. Wins all the time, naturally. And I hear he's the seventh son of a seventh son."

That did it. Dan had never met the seventh son of a seventh son and he's always wanted to. He was hooked. He demanded an introduction to the Marvel as soon as possible.

The next morning, about an hour before opening time, Dan unlocked the front door of Hoge's just as the customer was arriving with a dapper gentleman in a wasp-waisted, double-breasted suit. Locking the door again as soon as his companions were inside, he drew a large draft beer for the Marvel with a shot glass of Four Roses to keep it company. The Marvel drank both with the appreciation of a connoisseur and then sat down at one of the tables. He set up a traveling backgammon set and pulled a crystal sphere out of his overcoat pocket and set it down next to the game. Dan sat down opposite him after refilling the glasses.

As Dan told it to me later, the fellow was uncanny. It started with Dan's first roll, a three and a four. He reached out to make his moves but the Mental Marvel grabbed his sleeve and stopped him. The Marvel glanced into his crystal for a second or two and said, "I see it all!"

"What?"

"You were about to move these two men in this manner." And he moved two of Dan's men to new positions. Dan says he was astounded. It was a perfectly obvious move for early in the game and it was just the sort of move he *might* have made. In fact, there was nothing at all to prove that he wouldn't have made that move.

"By golly!" he said. The Mental Marvel smiled, revealing

expensively capped teeth and looked pointedly at the empty glasses. Dan refilled them.

And so it went. Dan says he never once touched the men. The Marvel saw in his crystal ball any move Dan was going to make or *probably* would have made. Sometimes Dan forged ahead and sometimes he dropped behind. He won the first game but as the play continued he (according to the Marvel) got overexcited. He began (the Marvel saw in his crystal) to make foolish moves. Dan says he ordinarily doesn't let backgammon get under his skin like that, and he very rarely makes foolish moves when there is considerable money riding on a game. But who was he to tell the Marvel what he saw in his very own crystal ball? This guy was a seventh son! He had powers!

"Oh dear!" said the Marvel as Dan wasted doubles to hit a blot that would have been better off going unhit. "I was hoping you wouldn't do that but the crystal never lies. And you're going to double, too."

"I am?" asked Dan.

"Unfortunately, yes," said the Marvel, "and I'll have to redouble."

"Do I accept?" Dan asked.

The Marvel peered into the ball again. "Yes, you do," he said.

A few rolls later, the Marvel bore the last man off the board and Dan lost a sixteen game at four dollars a point.

It was time to open the bar for the regular customers and the Marvel rose and said good-bye, pocketing his board and his crystal. He promised to return the next morning at the same time.

"I lost the money," Dan told me later, "but it was well worth it. What an experience! How many of us in this workaday world get to see Them at work?"

"Not many, thank God," I said.

In the following two weeks, Dan lost quite a bit more, including the small nest egg he'd been putting away to buy a motor boat for his place up at the lake. As the customer had told him, the Marvel always won, but Dan never tired of playing with him, shaking his head in wonder at the Marvel's feats of mind reading.

"Dan," I said, "if you'll listen to a few home truths from an old customer, I think this fellow is swindling you. You're an excellent player. You never would have made those stupid moves you always seem to make when you play with him or that he tells you you would have made. If you were left alone you'd probably beat him most of the time."

"But what about the crystal?" Dan wanted to know. "How can he see those moves in the crystal if I'm not going to make them?"

"He doesn't see anything in that crystal. He just *tells* you he does and you believe him. Have you ever seen anything in it?"

Dan had to admit he hadn't.

"Will you do me a favor, Dan?" I said. "Will you set up a game with the Mental Marvel for a friend of mine?"

No doubt the reader can guess who that friend was. For the purposes of this game, we enlisted the aid of Pat McNamara, the bartender of P. J. Murtagh's three blocks down the street. The match would be held there instead of at Hoge's.

Dan and I were already at Murtagh's when the Marvel arrived, armed with his board and a fine, keen thirst, which Pat proceeded to alleviate with one on the house. My friend, "Tom Kelly," soon appeared. It was, of course, Channing Bellinghast, dressed in the coveralls and tool belt of a telephone company lineman. The Marvel wiped his mouth, sized the newcomer up warily, smiled, and reached into his pocket for the crystal. A look of amazement spilled over his face. It wasn't there!

"Too bad," Bellinghast said. "I guess you won't be able to read my mind without it. I was counting on playing with you, too. It's payday, and I always get itchy on payday, unless there's a game somewhere. I guess I'll try some of the boys down at the firehouse."

"No! Wait a minute! Hold on!" the Marvel said. "I can read your mind without the crystal. At least, I think I can, if I concentrate hard. Of course, I might not play as well as I usually do, but I guess you won't mind that." He chuckled and waved his empty glass at Pat. Dan and I watched from the sidelines.

"I've got an idea," Pat said from behind the bar. "We're holding a crystal ball right here for a gypsy who left it one day when he couldn't pay for his drinks. He never came back for it. We keep it behind the bar as a kind of decoration." He pointed at a large object about the size of a bowling ball, standing on an ebony stand and made of clear glass. It nestled among the bottles behind the bar, softly lit by the indirect fluorescent lamps back there.

"Well, I don't know," the Marvel said. "A man likes his own crystal ball. I don't know about gypsies. Never trusted 'em very much." Then he smiled at Bellinghast. "I'll give it a try," he said, "just this once."

"No need to move it around," Pat said. "It weighs a ton. Why not play up here at the bar. Then you can watch it while you play. And what's more," and here he gave the Marvel a meaningful smile, "it'll be easier for me to get at the glasses when they're empty."

"Fine!" said the Marvel, and the game began. The dice rolled and he glanced at the globe behind the bar and then told Channing where he intended to move his men. Bellinghast didn't argue or disagree. Around about the fifth or sixth roll, the Marvel glanced at the crystal behind the bar and his face went deathly pale. He gulped and gulped again. He looked around at Dan and me and then up at

97

Pat, but Dan and I were quietly sipping our beers and Pat was mopping the bar surface with a rag. The Marvel moved two men to new positions with a shaking hand.

Bellinghast lost the first game and the second. The Marvel suggested raising the stakes and Channing agreed. He pulled a brown telephone company pay envelope out of his pocket and the Marvel reached into his shirt and brought out an oversized wallet, stuffed with ten and twenty dollar bills. He looked like a cat that has just eaten the fattest canary in town. He grinned at us and set up the men for a new game.

Halfway through the next game, he suddenly began to play wildly and eccentrically, making moves that made no sense at all. By the time Pat was ready to open the bar to the public, Bellinghast had taken away every penny the Marvel had on him. Dazed, the Marvel reeled out into the sunshine.

"Nothing to it," Channing said when he was gone. "I stole his crystal out of his pocket while Pat was giving him his first drink. Here it is." He placed it on the bar.

"But what happened?" I asked.

"You're probably too young to remember, like the Marvel," he said, grinning at Pat, who grinned back. "Back in the thirties and forties, the bars on the Loop in Chicago and on New York's Fifty-second Street used to advertise the Girl in the Fishbowl. It was a simple illusion. A pretty girl in a bathing suit sat in a room behind the bar. She was reflected in a series of mirrors down to a small mirror in a goldfish bowl, in such a way that it seemed she was only six inches high and actually inside the bowl. She would comb her hair and put on her makeup. The illusion was that this tiny creature actually lived in the bowl. The bar patrons knew it was only an illusion, but they loved it. Sometimes the girl would sing. Every now and then, she'd come out of the back room, full-sized, and take a bow, collecting tips all around. Like all gimmicks, it went out of fashion. The customers just got tired of it."

"Haven't seen it in forty years," Pat said. "Not since before the war."

At that moment, a pretty girl dressed in a long white robe, to the back of which was attached a pair of tinsel wings, appeared.

"Hi dad!" she said.

"Hi baby," Pat said. "Gentlemen, my daughter Maureen."

"Like all the older local bars, Murtagh's had the Girl in the Fishbowl years ago," Channing explained. "Pat and I merely cleaned out the back room, rearranged the mirrors, and got Maureen down here to help out."

"So the Marvel looked at the crystal, and for the first time in his life, he actually saw something in it?"

"Exactly. An angelic vision who followed the game move for move on a portable board and told him what to play. Since nobody else seemed to see the vision except him, he figured it was the real thing. Besides, he'd had a few, and Pat made sure they were triple strength. I might add that Maureen is the women's champion backgammon player of Indiana University."

"The Marvel had conned so many people into believing in his powers that he got to believing in them himself," Pat said. "It happens a lot. Mainly with politicians. I've seen it in this bar again and again."

"In order to be fooled by witches and fairies and Mental Marvels," Channing said, handing Dan the crystal for a souvenir, along with the money for his motor boat, "You've got to believe in them. If you don't believe, they can't hurt you. They just become ordinary people, like the Girl in the Fishbowl."

Dan nodded, but he didn't look happy. He'd gotten his money back, but he'd lost his illusions.

Channing's advice goes for you, too. Have fun with the supernatural, but keep your eyes open. As Len Deighton wrote, just because you don't believe in Santa Claus doesn't mean you have to shove your presents back up the chimney—but you don't have to lose any sleep staying up to listen for reindeer, either.

8
Happy Hustlers

At this point in time's continuum, we have pooled our knowledge about the pitfalls of careless play with small children, religious fanatics, Oriental spies, seers, and other difficult, shady, or downright dishonest adversaries.

A book like this one can only scratch the surface of backgammon villainy. Out there in the great world, there are varieties of rascality as yet undreamed of. Perhaps Channing Bellinghast, if and when he writes the auto-biography that so many publishers have begged him for, will unmask more of them than I can. He's certainly had the experience.

In general, I have always thought that the worst cheats of all are those who don't look it, who appear to be simple or-dinary folks. That nice young couple on the train, the pretty girl in the hotel lobby, the fellow from Cincinnati you met at the party. Salt of the earth, all of them, with innocent ex-pressions and wide, ingenuous smiles. Then one evening, they show their true colors. If you've let your guard drop, it can be expensive.

The world is full of hustlers. A hustler is easy enough to describe. Remember that girl who said she didn't know how to play and would you teach her and then took you for two hundred dollars? You were hustled. Don't forget what happened to young Betty Carrington, head of her class at Wellesley and a member of MENSA. Betty ran into a self-styled Russian grand master who claimed he could play an entire game of backgammon without using men! He put aside all the pieces and rolled the dice, memorizing each move that would have transpired on the empty board.

Betty says she was able to remember where his men and hers were supposed to be situated for the first five rolls. Then she got confused, but he was so pompous about it that she wasn't about to tell him she couldn't remember, so she pretended. He kept hitting blots she didn't know she had and finally came through with a triumphant gammon. She was too proud to complain. She was hustled.

Don't forget that in nineteenth-century England, the slang word "to gammon" meant to swindle. And that brings us to a special form of cozening that was practiced on some friends of mine.

The Federal Felon Fabrication

A weekend in Southampton at the Hillman's is always an experience. Dorsey Hillman is, by my standards, a rich man. Briefly stated, my standards include: ownership of a Rolls Royce, two homes, and enough unearned income to remove the need for holding down a nine-to-five job.

The Hillmans' summer place, not to be confused with their enormous apartment in Manhattan overlooking the East River, is within walking distance of the Atlantic Ocean. It boasts five or six acres of expensive, neatly barbered and landscaped real estate, and a rambling house with innum-

erable rooms containing comfortable, unostentatious furniture. Weekends there are pleasantly informal and the
food is excellent. Meals are prepared by old servants who
have been with the family for many years under the super-
vision of Dorsey's wife, Millie. Although she can well afford
to leave household matters to paid helpers, Millie has not
lost interest in her kitchen. At mealtimes, her virtuosity
shows in the quality and variety of the dishes served.

The central item of furniture in the Hillmans' small
sitting-room-cum-library is a commodious backgammon
table, set up ready for play with its veined green and black
marble men in position, the dice cups on their marks for
anyone who wants to try a game. The table is placed so that
the players can either sit on chairs or recline comfortably on
sofas at right angles to one another. It is the table of an enthusiast, not just for show or occasional casual amusement,
but for the serious occupation of players devoted to the
game.

Dorsey and I have spent a good deal of time facing each
other across that table, locked in mortal combat. He is a
good, steady player, not quite as good as he thinks he is,
but a fine strategist and a dangerous man with a power
cube.

On the fine morning, which began the episode on which
this chapter is based, Dorsey, an early riser, was already up
and sitting in the drawing room enjoying a cup of Millie's excellent coffee when I came in to join him. It was a Sunday,
always a sad day in the season, because it means the end of
a weekend and the necessity, for me at any rate, of return-
ing to the hot city from the pleasant seashore. But even the
spectre of New York's Long Island Rail Road could not
depress me on such a lovely morning. I greeted my host,
poured myself a cup of coffee, and sat down on the sofa
nearest the window that overlooked the garden.

Dorsey was sorting through several days' mail, segregating bills and letters, occasionally tearing one open to read it. As I watched him, he slit an evelope with his letter opener and removed its contents. I could see that it was not a bill but a personal missive, somewhat grubby and written in a sprawling handwriting. He read it with great attention and then, suddenly, uttered a cry of impatience, crumpled the letter into a ball, and tossed it into a porcelain frog that served as a wastebasket.

"Bad news?" I asked.

"No. Nothing. Just irritating, that's all."

He got up and walked across the room to a desk from whose drawer he drew a checkbook. He wrote out a check, scribbled a quick note, and put them into an envelope, sealing the flap and addressing it. From my place on the sofa I could not see the address, but that was not necessary, for he got up and handed the envelope to me.

"Would you mind mailing this when you get to the city this afternoon?" he asked. "It takes ages for mail to get anywhere from Southampton."

I pocketed the letter and assured him that I didn't mind in the least.

Millie had come in during this short dialogue. She saw the expression on his face, the open checkbook, and the letter he had handed to me.

"Oh Dorsey! Not again!" she said, smiling.

"Yes, again. And it's not funny. But I'm getting closer. It was neck and neck this time."

"Close doesn't count in backgammon. You win or you lose. There are no gray areas," Millie said, putting a fresh pot of coffee and a rack of hot toast on the table.

I confess I was consumed with curiosity. The mysterious check sputtered in my pocket like a firecracker. I was dying to pull the letter out and look at the address. Dorsey munched his toast thoughtfully, showing no sign of discussing the matter further.

That afternoon, safely settled in a parlor car roomette, I pulled out the letter to see who the addressee might be. Written in Dorsey's neat, authoritative hand, was the name Harlowe Wentworth, followed by a number, 1040681. Obviously a military man. But no! I was astounded on reading further to see that the address was the federal penitentiary in Lewisburg, Pennsylvania!

Dorsey Hillman corresponding with a convicted criminal! And sending him money? What on earth could be behind this bizarre circumstance? I was completely nonplussed. The only answer to the riddle was Millie. Dorsey had been put out by the message in the letter he'd received, but Millie had been amused. Maybe she would be less reluctant to tell the story than her husband. I knew she was in the habit of coming to town for a day or two each week, and as soon as I got home, I dialed her Southampton number and dragooned her into a luncheon date, just the two of us, at Chetwode's.

"What is it?" she wanted to know when we had finished our drinks and the clams had been served.

"What is what?"

"You know what. You aren't about to invite a respectable married woman to an expensive lunch, here of all places, unless you want something. Obviously it's not my body. What is it?"

"I should have known better than to try to fool you."

"It's the letter, isn't it?"

I nodded.

"Well," Millie said, laughing, "it isn't really that much of a mystery. Dorsey heard about Harlowe Wentworth through a mutual acquaintance. He's doing a year at Lewisburg for nonpayment of alimony. He couldn't pay because his business failed. You can bet that won Dorsey's approval and sympathy at once. He's still supporting Edna in the style of a grand duchess. While Wentworth is serving his time, he whiles away the boredom by playing backgammon by mail with a top-ranking player. Dorsey was very flattered when Wentworth accepted his application."

"His application?"

"Yes. He's terribly exclusive. The application form went very deeply into Dorsey's background."

"I see. So Dorsey was accepted by this fellow. But how do they play?"

"They write to each other. Each letter contains that day's moves, scores, and dice combinations."

"And Dorsey was upset Sunday morning when he read Wentworth's letter because he lost?"

"Right. Wentworth wrote that he'd thrown double fives and taken off his last three men. It was a gammon doubled, I think."

"Good heavens! You mean Dorsey believed him? He actually accepted a convict's word about an invisible roll of the dice and sent him money on the strength of it?"

"Don't be such an old curmudgeon. It isn't as though Wentworth were a criminal. His vicious, sadistic ex-wife crucified him because he was broke. It could happen to anybody. Besides, he mentioned in one of his letters that he'd been a member of the Brook Club and the Society of the Two World Wars. You know what a war buff Dorsey is, with his PT boats and all that. Wentworth was in the navy, too. Destroyers."

"Did he tell Dorsey that before or after he saw Dorsey's application form?"

"Oh don't be so suspicious," Millie said, waving to the waiter for another Punt é Mes. "You've forgotten how things are done among gentlemen since that swami in Hong

Kong conned you. I heard all about that. Your friend Channing Bellinghast has been filling your head with a lot of horror stories. That's what's wrong with you."

I suppose she could have been right. Maybe I was over-suspicious, but just in case, I phoned my old friend Lieutenant Larry Dempsey of the New York Police Department's backgammon squad. A week later he called me back.

"Got it all right here," he said. "Your friend Wentworth, alias 'Dancing Dan' O'Shea, alias 'Sleeves' Donahue, alias 'Handsome Harry' Boatwright, is very well-known to our computer. He's got a record as long as your arm."

"You mean he's defaulted on his alimony before?"

"Alimony nothing! He's doing five to ten for securities fraud. It's his third offense. They don't have alimony cases at Lewisburg. It's a federal penitentiary."

"Securities fraud! Then he's not a gentleman after all?"

"Hardly. After you phoned me, I tipped the warden to put a watch on his mail. Your friend Hillman isn't his only pigeon. He's been playing by mail with fifty of them simultaneously, each one thinking he's the only one. They're all over the country. His weekly take has been in the thousands, or it was until they lowered the boom on him yesterday."

Double fives and gammon indeed! Dorsey, however, did not seemed pleased when I broke the news, apparently regarding me as a busybody, an attitude I found it hard not to resent. Millie didn't stop laughing for twenty minutes.

Wentworth was charged with thirty-two counts of mail fraud and extortion, but he beat all of them. For some reason, the district attorney couldn't get anyone (including Dorsey) to testify.

As you can see, the way to beat hustlers is to outhustle them or, failing that, to send them to jail, unless they hap-

107

pen to be there already. In that case I don't know what to advise. You're on your own. Obviously, Dorsey and his co-victims got exactly what they deserved and so might you unless you're careful.

In these pages I have done my best to expose for you a number of backgammon scoundrels of all species. Some are hateful creatures, deserving the most severe and brutal punishments known to man. Others are lovable but weak. All are worthy of close scrutiny, for who knows, one of them might one day be sitting across the table from you, rattling the dice cup preparatory to slicing you into small, neat pieces.

Backgammon bandits can easily be segregated into categories (although some outstanding ones are unique and don't fit into any category at all, but these are exceptions). Everyone who plays regularly runs across these monsters from time to time, all over the civilized world. If and when life is discovered on other planets, we'll probably find them out there, too.

Of course, as I have remarked earlier herein, it is hard to cheat at backgammon because the game is so simple and logical that winning is a combination of skill and luck. You can't mark the pieces like cards, because they all have the same value and they all look alike. You can't load the dice because you don't know what combination you might need and an abundance of doubles would soon be obvious to your opponent.

Therefore, the easiest way to help one's luck along and compensate for lack of skill is not to manipulate the equipment but to rattle your opponents. To shake and disorient them until they can't make the decisions necessary for victorious play. Under normal conditions, a calm, easygoing player will usually win over an opponent who is choking with rage, paralyzed with fear, or undergoing a partial nervous breakdown. Take, for example, my friend Dale Miller, a passionate devotee of the game who plays every chance she gets. This sort of enthusiasm naturally reduces the opportunity for careful screening of one's opponents. Dale says she's played with a number of very odd birds indeed, but the ones that irritated her the most she groups under the heading Nervous Types.

Backgammon Gastronomique

Nervous Types always prepare for a game like the late Admiral Richard E. Byrd preparing for an expedition to the North Pole. They arm themselves with enough food to provision three African villages for a month. They have chocolate bars, peanuts, pretzels, soda pop, six-packs of beer, hard and soft candies, Fritos, Oreos, and a sandwich or two. And just to make sure their jaws have something to do when the food is all consumed, they add a plentiful supply of chewing gum.

That takes care of their oral needs, covering the area above the neck and below the nose. But what about the rest of them? Their sinuses, for instance. In addition to edibles, they lay in a comfortable supply of Kleenex, nose drops, and a Benzedrine inhaler, which they persistently imbed in their nostrils, wheezing heavily.

And let's not forget the extremities. While the jaws are occupied and the mucous membranes are being freeze-dried, they aren't about to let the rest of the body enjoy a well-earned rest. Oh no. While you're rolling the dice and trying to concentrate on the game, they drum their fingers impatiently on the table. They tap their feet up and down as though they were pedalling the mighty organs that were built into Loew's movie theatres in the twenties. They wriggle until their chairs creak and groan in protest. They shuffle and shift and rattle and bang and rap and honk and whistle and hum.

When they stop for a minute to catch a breath, the silence is so deafening that it irritates even more than the noise did.

Dale says she avoids these people as a rule, but sometimes she can't escape them for one reason or another. When you find yourself trapped at a table with a Nervous Type, Dale advises, you can defeat them at their own game in two ways.

First, you can outjitter them. Unfortunately, that takes a lot of energy. When she is faced with the prospect of playing with a munching, wheezing, rapping ditherer, Dale says she supplies herself with a stockpile of ammunition of her own. She has had designed for her a special kind of saltine that pops with a loud snap when bitten, spraying the table with whitish crumbs. She has discovered a little-known kind of South American bubble gum that blows bubbles of enormous size that shatter with a loud report, settling onto the board and covering it with sticky, pink chicle. With these for starters, she then moves onto a meal of utterly disgusting foodstuffs.

She beings with *ch'ou tou fu,* a kind of fermented bean curd imported from Taiwan, where it can be smelled three blocks away when the peddler moves through the streets with his pushcart. She garnishes this with Korean *kimshi,* which smells worse. She follows up with some of the better-known Italian and German cheeses. The tropical fruit called durian is her dessert. It has a smell guaranteed to nauseate anyone within noseshot. Dale, of course, is careful to block her own nostrils in advance with wads of cotton dipped in eau de cologne.

She tells me she once had remarkable success in reducing an adversary to semi-idiocy by dipping crackers into chopped chicken liver mixed with hard boiled egg, unobtrusive in itself but highly disturbing when eaten from a 9-Lives Cat Food can.

As an adjunct to these items, she provides herself with a brass spittoon and a plug of Red Apple chewing tobacco. By stepping on a remote-control pedal, she is able to make the spittoon go "plink" every time she pretends to spit in its direction. The tobacco, of course, can be replaced with shredded licorice whips.

If you can't outchew, outdither, or outjitter them, there is still the second method. If playing in one of those mechanical reducing devices that consists of a vibrating belt around your bottom doesn't work, Dale says, the thing to do is retain an icy calm, ignoring all their fooleries. Sound impossible? Not if you put away a pint of good brandy in advance, or, if you prefer, three valiums.

That should prepare you for everything. Then, if you run into a backgammon bore or rascal, you won't mind a bit. In fact, you might even learn to enjoy it.

9
And More Rabbits

As I have pointed out in various places supra, this book has been written to instruct. It is not, strictly speaking, a how-to manual or an explanation of the techniques and intricacies of the game. We can assume that you already know the required basics—or how would you have progressed this far? Skill is not all, for what good is technical artistry when you find yourself at the mercy of a fishy-eyed Chic Sheikh or a determined (and bewitching) young Jill-the-Ripper? No matter how adept you may be, would your knowledge protect you from the peanut-butter-and-jelly-smeared machinations of a Mendacious Midget? No indeed!

My lessons are aimed not at teaching you how to play but at teaching you to avoid losing. And, as Zen Master T'ang has pointed out on numerous occasions, he who avoids losing, wins.

If you've been paying attention, you have by this time stored away a quiverful of backhanded and somewhat questionable tactics calculated to bemuse any scalawag aiming to pilfer your watch and shatter your savoir faire across a game table. But just in case, here are a few last effort dirty tricks to use when your back is to the wall and Channing Bellinghast is off on his annual Canadian salmon-fishing holiday beyond the reach of a telephone.

The African Snail Artifice

Under normal conditions a game of backgammon takes between six and twelve minutes. A player's blood pressure will rise and fall with the pace and rhythm of the play. But suppose you were able to slow down that pace and rhythm, to delay the game indefinitely. Suppose your adversary were of a temperament of the sort usually described as a "bundle of nerves." See the possibilities?

As a start, try allotting five minutes for each move. Study the dice carefully when they emerge from the cup. Count each combination on your fingers, moving your lips with the numbers as you contemplate the possible moves. Track each allowable alternative with your index finger. Consult a backgammon book, taking your time about finding the proper page. Then, finally, when your blue-lipped opponent is stifling a primal scream, move your man.

Between moves disappear from the room for long periods of time, offering as an excuse only a mumbled, unintelligible apology. You can use your absence to advantage. Catch up on your correspondence. Make that long-forgotten phone call to your mother. Clean out the attic. Build a model airplane. Vacuum the upstairs carpet.

In the meantime your opponent will be waiting for you, turning alternately dark red and ashy pale. His temples will throb. His hands will clench and unclench. His breathing will become rapid and irregular. At the critical moment, come back to the table and reach for the doubling cube. You can't lose.

The Helpful-Hannah Hoax

This form of attack is based on the creation of a fine rapport with your adversary, in which you represent yourself as his closest friend, a well-wisher with only your opponent's best interests at heart. As soon as the board is set up and it is time to roll for first play, you make it plain that in this game your purpose is to *help*. You mean to give your opponent a few salient pointers which will make him a better player and consequently a better human being.

It will not, of course, be lost on your opposition that if you are prepared to help or teach, you must consider yourself superior in every way. Helping is a classic put down. You're a step ahead even before the dice have been rolled.

Carry on from there. "Aha!" you shout, as your opponent rolls a double. "Duplicate arrivals!" Explain in detail how doubles are better than other combinations because you get extra moves, waving away the protestations that he already knows about that. Whatever you may roll after your opponent's doubles, explain that you have produced "Ratberger's Response," a seventeenth-century gambit favored by Louis XIII. Inform the player that this calls for "The Memison Expectancy," which is, of course, however you choose to place your men according to the combination thrown.

Point out every single blot, slowly and distinctly, as though you were talking to a very small child. Imply that but for your assistance he would probably overlook half a dozen vulnerable men, missing opportunities for winning moves, not out of *stupidity*, mind you, just out of carelessness.

Meanwhile, carry on an off-the-board razzle-dazzle aimed at chipping away whatever is left of his sanity. If he smokes say that you're allergic to tobacco fumes. If he drinks serve him diet cola and tell him you're on the Dr. Atkins diet. If he has a train to catch, announce the time every five minutes. "Only three hundred and seventeen minutes to go," you cry cheerfully as he nervously consults his watch and tries to concentrate on the game.

Don't despair if it doesn't work right away. Just keep it up and sooner or later he'll crack. And then all you have to do is pick up the pieces.

Yawning Becomes Electra

Remember Lauren Bacall in her early films, the absolute insouciance, the unshakable, impregnable boredom with which she greeted disasters of all kinds? Miss Bacall typifies a breed of backgammon bunco artist known as the Bored Type. There are few experiences more debilitating than playing against a Bored Type. A stiff siege of infectious hepatitis may be a little worse, but even that is doubtful.

To the Bored Type, the game of backgammon and the opponent sitting across the table are as dust beneath his chariot wheels. These monsters can make even the most exciting match seem dull. They droop languidly over the board, stifling an occasional yawn, looking pointedly at their watches as though there were nothing in the world so conducive to ennui as a game with you. Eventually you'll begin yawning too. The conviction will seep into your brain that if somebody finds you that boring to play with, you must *be* that boring to play with. Your eyelids will descend to half-mast and hang there loosely. You'll fidget. At last, when you're practically inert, your adversary will suddenly perk up and win the game.

The Bored Type will resort to a number of nasty little tricks to defeat you. If your bored opponent is a woman, she'll bring along an intricate needlepoint pattern and work on it as she plays or she'll knit an argyll sock. She may wheel in the TV and watch an old movie or carry on a long telephone conversation with a friend as she rolls the dice and moves her men. If it is a male across the table, he may negotiate a business deal or give instructions to his broker while he plays, using the hand that isn't busy with the phone.

A friend of mine (who has asked me to withhold her name so she won't become a cult figure) has been burned a few times by Bored Types and has figured out a few strategems of her own to counteract their soporific effect. To beat them at their own game, she says, just pay less attention to the game than they do.

On one occasion, she reports, when the game was at her house, she confounded her Bored Type opponent by having herself wheeled in on a table wrapped in a sheet. During the game, she underwent a complete home diathermy treatment, electrolysis for removal of unwanted hair, and a pedicure for elimination of dead skin and unsightly callouses, rolling the dice all the while by holding the dice cup in her mouth.

On another occasion a nurse appeared in mid game, tied off her arm, and withdrew a pint of blood for donation to a local hospital's plasma bank.

You can bet her Bored Type opponent stopped being bored. The best part of both of these strategems was that in addition to winning she ended up looking much better and earned a free glass of orange juice from the hospital too.

See how simple it is? Just keep one thing paramount in your mind at all times. When you're playing backhanded backgammon, it doesn't matter how you play the game, it's whether you win or lose.